Instant Pot Pressure Cooker Cookbook

Yummy

Best Instant Pot Receipes for Beginners and Advanced Users - Have a Happy Healthy Life

Shanice Johnson

INTRODUCTION	**6**
CHAPTER ONE: SIMPLE AND QUICK SOLUTIONS AS TO HOW TO USE YOUR INSTANT POT EFFECTIVELY	**8**
What Is An Instant Pot?	8
Benefits of an Instant Pot	8
Tips to Increase Instant Pot's Efficiency	10
How to Clean an Instant Pot?	12
For everyday cleaning	*12*
For deep cleaning	*12*
CHAPTER TWO: INSTANT POT BREAKFAST RECIPES	**14**
Instant Pot Vegan Breakfast Recipes	14
Chocolate Steel Cut Oats	14
Cornmeal Polenta Porridge	14
Toasted Granola	15
Breakfast Quinoa with Blueberries and Bananas	16
Cranberry Apple Oatmeal	17
French toast Casserole	17
Coconut Quinoa Breakfast Bowl	18
Pumpkin Coffeecake Steel-cut Oatmeal	19
Brown Rice Porridge	19
Banana Bread Instant Pot Steel Cut Oats	20
Breakfast Instant Pot Pie with Sausage and Beans	21
Sprouted Lentils Breakfast Bowl	22
Miso Breakfast Oats	23
Cilantro Lime Quinoa	24
Japanese Breakfast Sweet Potatoes	24
Low Carb Breakfast Recipes	25
Omelet Bites	25
Mediterranean Breakfast Casserole	26
Healthy Egg Muffins	27
Broccoli Ham and Pepper Frittata	28
Egg Cheese Bake	29
Chili and Cheese Frittata	30
Breakfast Casserole	30
Omelet Casserole	31
Blueberry Muffins	32
Crustless Meaty Quiche	33

OMELET QUICHE	34
SCOTCH EGGS	35
LOW CARB EGG BENEDICT	36
COCONUT LOW CARB PORRIDGE	37
SERVES: 3	37
BANANA NUT BREAD	38

CHAPTER THREE: INSTANT POT SOUP RECIPES — 40

CHEESY CAULIFLOWER SOUP	40
BLACK BEAN SOUP	41
BEEF AND MACARONI SOUP	41
CREAMY CHICKEN AND MUSHROOM SOUP	42
BUTTERNUT SQUASH SOUP	44
CHICKEN "NOODLE" SOUP	45
LASAGNA SOUP (BEEF/ VEGETARIAN)	46
CARNITAS SOUP	47

CHAPTER FOUR: INSTANT POT VEGAN RECIPES — 48

TEMPEH, POTATO AND KALE BOWL — 48

VEGAN QUINOA BURRITO BOWLS	49
VEGETABLE AND TOFU CURRY	50
PERSIAN CHICKPEA STEW	51
VEGAN SPAGHETTI	52
CAULIFLOWER BOLOGNESE WITH ZUCCHINI NOODLES	53
PUMPKIN WALNUT CHILI	54

CHAPTER FIVE: INSTANT POT POULTRY RECIPES — 55

CHICKEN BURRITO BOWLS	56
CHICKEN POT PIE	56
HAWAIIAN BARBEQUE CHICKEN	57
SALSA LIME CHICKEN	58
TERIYAKI CHICKEN AND RICE	60
CHILI LIME CHICKEN	61
TURKEY QUINOA BOWLS	62
TURKEY BREAST WITH GRAVY	63

CHAPTER SIX: INSTANT POT MEAT RECIPES — 64

TACO CASSEROLE	64
HAMBURGER STEW	65
ITALIAN BEEF	66

Apricot Glazed Pork Roast	66
Sweet Pulled Pork	67
Apple Cider Pork Loin	67
Carnitas Tacos	68
Indian Ground Lamb Curry	69

CHAPTER SEVEN: LOW CARB LUNCH RECIPES — 70

Shredded Pork with Beans	70
Beef and Mushroom Stew	70
Creamy Cauliflower Soup	71
Poblano Chicken Soup	72
Bacon Cheddar and Broccoli Salad	73
Egg Salad	73
Spinach Frittata	74

CHAPTER EIGHT: INSTANT POT NOODLE RECIPES — 76

Beef and Spaghetti	76
Mac and Cheese	77
Asian Noodle Bowls	77
Spaghetti and Meatballs	78
Chicken Alfredo	79
Enchilada Pasta	79
Chicken Sausage Pasta	80
Broccoli & Cheddar Pasta	81

CHAPTER NINE: INSTANT POT VEGETARIAN RECIPES — 82

Creamed Corn	82
Enchilada Quinoa	83
Instant Pot Rice and Beans	83
Peas Risotto	84
Vegetarian Chili	85
Chipotle-Orange Broccoli & Tofu	85
Coconut Curry	86

CHAPTER TEN: INSTANT POT SEAFOOD RECIPES — 87

Beer Potato Fish	87
Fish with Orange and Ginger Sauce	87
Garlic Butter Tilapia	88
Peas with Cod	89
Sweet and Sour Shrimp	90
Spicy Mussels in Tomato Gravy	90

CHAPTER ELEVEN: INSTANT SNACKS RECIPES — 92

- BBQ Chicken Drummies — 92
- Asian Chinese Boiled Peanuts — 93
- Five Spice Chicken Wings — 93
- Lettuce Wraps — 94
- Corn on the Cob — 95
- BBQ Smoked Sausage — 95
- Cocktail Meatballs — 96
- Chicken Nachos — 97
- Little Smokies — 98
- Garlic and Butter Mushrooms — 98
- Instant Pot Popcorns — 99
- Queso Dip — 100
- Spinach and Artichoke Dip — 100
- Buffalo Chicken Dip — 101
- Sausage Dip — 101

CHAPTER TWELVE: INSTANT POT DESSERT RECIPES — 103

- Blueberry Pudding — 103
- Chai Spiced Pears — 104
- Chocolate Fudge — 104
- Pineapple Cake — 105
- Raspberry Curd — 106
- Chocolate Fondue — 107
- Quick Custard — 107
- Crème Brulee — 108
- Fruit Cake — 109
- Winter Fruit Compote — 109

CHAPTER THIRTEEN: INSTANT POT LOW CARB DESSERTS — 111

- Thai Coconut Pandan Custard — 111
- Coffee Roll Egg Custard — 111
- Peanut Butter Chocolate Cheesecake — 112
- Vanilla Bean Cheesecake — 113

CONCLUSION — 114

Introduction

Do you want to whip up tasty food without spending hours together in the kitchen? Well, this is indeed possible if you start using the Instant Pot. The Instant Pot is a fantastic kitchen appliance, which is quite simple to use. It helps save time as well as effort when it comes to cooking. An Instant Pot uses pressurized steam to cook food and helps seal the nutrients present in the food. It performs all the functions of a slow cooker, an electric pressure cooker, a yogurt maker, a rice cooker, steamer, sautéing pan, and a warming pot as well.

In this book, you will find specific helpful tips and tricks to make the most of the Instant Pot along with the cleaning procedure. If you like the idea of quick and convenient cooking, then this appliance will come in handy. All that you need to do is set it and then forget about it until your food is fully cooked.

In this book, you will find different recipes that you can cook using the Instant Pot. You don't need a variety of kitchen appliances, and this one appliance will do the work for you. All the recipes given in this book are not only easy to cook, but quite delicious as well. From appetizers to desserts, you can cook a perfect meal using the instant pot. Instant Pot is an investment that keeps on giving. So, what are you waiting for? Let us get started immediately.

Chapter One: Simple and Quick Solutions as to How to Use Your Instant Pot Effectively

What Is An Instant Pot?

To thoroughly learn about cooking using an Instant Pot, it is essential to understand what an Instant Pot means. Instant Pot is a brand of multipurpose appliance that has become quite popular because they help save time as well as space in the kitchen. Instead of investing in a variety of appliances, all that you need to invest in is an instant pot. An Instant Pot can function as a pressure cooker, along with a couple of other appliances.

Pressure-cooking is the easiest and quickest way to get food to the table. Regardless of whether it is an electric pressure cooker or a classic stovetop pressure cooker, pressure-cooking drastically reduces the cooking time by increasing the boiling point of water and trapped in this team. Once the food is cooked, you can either wait for this team to release itself naturally or release the pressure manually by releasing the knob. Slow cookers come in handy if you like the idea of having a hot meal waiting for you at home. They are the "set it and forget it," appliances.

Benefits of an Instant Pot

In this section, you will learn about the different benefits of using an instant pot.

Pressure-cooking helps save time as well as energy. The time taken to cook food in an Instant Pot is lower than using any other conventional methods of cooking. Since you don't need much water while cooking in an instant cooker, the energy required is also quite less. When compared to conventional cooking techniques like boiling steaming while cooking on the stovetop, and Instant Pot helps save energy.

Pressure-cooking helps ensure that the heat is spread evenly and quickly. You don't have submerged the ingredients and water, but ensure that there is sufficient water to create steam within the inner pot. All the nutrients present in food, such as minerals and vitamins, stay intact during the cooking process. Food cooked in an Instant Pot will not be oxidized by air or direct exposure to heat, and therefore even fresh greens will retain the color after cooking.

The unique sealing mechanism helps ensure that all the food odors along with steam don't exit the instant pot. It makes for a clean and extremely convenient cooking appliance. Because of the cooking cycle is controlled by microprocessors and an instant pot, you can ensure consistency in cooking. Any cut of meat can also be cooked to perfection using this appliance. For instance, pork belly can be cooked in it, and once the meat is sufficiently cooked, the board will separate from the meat. Pressure-cooking can also be used to cook whole grains and other beans as well.

An Instant Pot has different operation buttons that perform various cooking tasks like cooking rice, sautéing, making soups, cooking poultry, meat, and stews, steaming, slow cooking, keeping warm, or even making you got. Each of the function buttons on the Instant Pot helps achieve consistent results.

For instance, the rice button helps the Instant Pot estimate the amount of rice and water by measuring the preheating time. The duration of the pressure-cooking will change according to this measurement and the stage of cooking. Each of these function buttons can be further refined by varying the range of the food from red to well down according to your preferences.

The automatic cooking function offered by it is quite convenient. Once the food is cooked, it will turn off the cooking process and switch on to keeping the food warm. Unlike a conventional pressure cooker, you don't have to stand and continuously monitor the cooking time in the process. The slow cooking is another brilliant feature of the instant pot. It means that you can plan your meals well ahead of time. You don't have to wait for the meal to be ready. It means that your cooking time is reduced by more than half because of all this.

A lot of people shy away from cooking because of the cleaning involved. You don't have to worry about cleaning a bunch of dishes, and all that you need clean is the Instant Pot. Since the inner pot is firmly sealed, you don't have to worry about any food aromas slipping out of the pot. Also, cleaning one dish is undoubtedly much more straightforward than having to clean a variety of them.

Since the food cooked in an Instant Pot is cooked at a temperature above the boiling point of water, it helps get rid of any harmful microorganisms present. Pressure-cooking is a great way to start sterilizing the food you consume. It is not just healthy, but also nutritious.

Tips to Increase Instant Pot's Efficiency

From cooking tough cuts of meat to frozen foods, you can pretty much cook anything in an instant pot. Chuck all the ingredients into the pot, press the required button, and wait for it to work its magic. However, if you want to make the most out of your Instant Pot and cook delicious meals, then there are a couple of things you can do to increase its efficiency. In this section, you will learn about the best tips and tricks you can use to make the most of your Instant Pot.

Whenever you want to pressure cook anything in the instant pot, ensure that you use at least half a cup of liquid water. Since a pressure cooker uses steam to cook, then needs to be sufficient steam building up within. To create this kind of pressure, the inner pot needs at least half a cup of liquid. Never skip this step, especially if you're using the pressure cooker function of the instant pot.

You can use any liquid and don't restrict yourself to water. Using flavorful liquids such as juices, stocks, and broths can add extra flavor to the meals you cook. Even basic rice can be jazzed up by using a little broth instead of plain water. If you're cooking chicken, opt for chicken broth instead of regular water.

Different functions and buttons are corresponding to these functions present on the instant pot. Don't be under the impression that you can only use one button whenever you cook. According to the recipe you wish to follow, vary the functions you use. For instance, you can start with the sauté button to caramelize the ingredients during the initial stages of cooking. Then you can shift to the pressure-cooking button. Once the food is ready, you don't immediately have to shift it to another container. Instead, you can leave it in the Instant Pot itself by pressing the Keep Warm function button.

A lot of people believe that once they select a function, that's all, there is to an instant pot. However, you can also adjust the temperature of the Instant Pot while using the sauté or slow cooker functions. By doing this, you can ensure that the temperature suits those specific ingredients you are trying to cook or the recipe you are following. Some dishes require a high temperature while others don't.

If you pressure cooking anything in the instant pot, then ensure that you add ten extra minutes to the entire meal preparation time. The Instant Pot takes about 10 minutes to develop the necessary pressure within the inner pot. So, while using any of the pressure buttons, add at least 10 to 15 extra minutes of cooking time. For instance, if the pot roast requires 40 minutes, then the meal will be ready between 50 to 55 minutes.

The Instant Pot is an extremely safe kitchen appliance; however, this is not a reason to ignore common sense. There are basic safety measures you must take, especially while cooking in a pressure mode. If you are manually releasing the pressure off of the Instant Pot by shifting the sealing valve, then hot steam will be released from the instant pot. Therefore, stay away from the Instant Pot while doing this. At least maintain some distance and don't put your face directly in the path of this steam.

You can easily and quickly cook meals using the instant pot. According to the size and the cart of the meets you are using along with whether they are frozen or fresh ones, the time taken will vary. You can cook most of the vegetables within five minutes while certain root vegetables like beetroots and potatoes might require a while longer. So, learn to change the cooking time according to the ingredients you are using. After all, overcooked or undercooked food is barely appetizing.

The inner pot is one of the most critical aspects of an instant pot. Therefore, ensure that you have at least one extra inner pot always ready. By doing this, you can cook multiple dishes in a single cooking session without having to clean the inner pot after every dish you prepare. Not just the inner pot, but ensure that you have a couple of extra sealing ring is present as well. The ceiling ring helps trap the flavor as well as the steam within the instant pot. So, at times, flavors and aromas from the food you cook tent to get absorbed by the sealing ring. Keep a specific sealing ring for savory items and another one for desserts. If you don't want the cheesecake, you cook to smell of chili you made the other night, then use two separate sealing rings.

Most of the instant pots come along with a yogurt making function. Having said that, the Instant Pot isn't always the best appliance to make creamy or cheesy sauces. Milk tends to scalp rather easily while cheese can congeal or become watery if you aren't careful. If you are cooking with dairy, ensure that you are paying close attention to the cooking process. Also, add the dairy products only after the pressure-cooking function ends. If not, you might end up with cheese sauce splattered all across your kitchen counter.

A great thing about Instant Pot is that it can retain liquid even after the cooking process. It isn't always a good thing, especially if you end up with a final dish that is too watery or runny. So, be prepared to thicken the tissue cook, if it has a little too much liquid in it. The simplest way to fix this is by adding a mixture of cornstarch and water by adding a little slurry after the cooking process thickens up the dish.

The inner pot, steam rack, and other non-electronic components of an Instant Pot can go directly into the dishwasher. It means cleaning becomes quite easy. The outer surface of the report can be easily wiped down using a wet towel, and the same applies to the lid as well. You will learn more about cleaning the Instant Pot in the next section.

Most of the popular Instant Pot models tend to have a steaming rack. You can use this to steam vegetables. However, there is more to it than just steaming vegetables. Whenever you want to cook an ingredient without allowing it to come in contact with the liquid present at the bottom of the pot, use a steaming rack. This comes in handy while cooking hard-boiled eggs or making desserts.

Don't be scared to experiment with different cooking functions present in the instant pot. Start with the preset ones and vary the temperature and cooking time according to the recipes. Also, spend some time and explore the different features of the instant pot. The Instant Pot is truly a magical appliance that makes cooking seem like a breeze. By following the different recipes given in this book, you can whip up delicious and nutritious meals within no time. What more? You can do all this without worrying about cleaning a pile of dishes later.

How to Clean an Instant Pot?

Instant pot certainly makes your life more comfortable in the kitchen. However, as with any other kitchen appliance, you must clean the Instant Pot after every use. In this section, you will learn about tips to regularly clean your Instant Pot, along with the steps to deep clean it.

For everyday cleaning

Start by washing the inner pot. You can load it in your regular dishwasher along with other dishes. To wipe the inside as well as outside of the cocoa, use a wet dishcloth. After every use, clean the silicone ring present on the inside of the lid. By doing this, you can prevent it from picking on any of the colors or odors from the food you cook. It can also be safely washed in the dishwasher. While cleaning, don't forget the inside of the lid. Wash it like you would wash any other regular dishes.

For deep cleaning

To prevent any unnecessary clogging, remove any food smells, or even stubborn food stains from forming, you must deep clean the Instant Pot at least once a month. Deep clean it more than this if you use it rather frequently. Here are the steps you can follow.

Before you start cleaning it, always unplug the instant pot. This is incredibly important, especially if you are deep cleaning it. The second step is to start cleaning the housing unit. Use a ramp and a clean rag for wiping down the inside as well as outside of the housing unit. The housing unit is the main part of the cooker of the instant pot. If you notice any dried food residues, then use a small brush to brush them away. Ensure that you clean all the nooks and crannies of this cooker. The third step is to start washing the lid. You can use regular dish soap to clean the lid. Wash it the way you would clean dishes.

The fourth step is to check all the smaller parts of the instant pot. It is where food or even other residues start forming. Start by removing the quick release handle and then pulled straight up to open it. Use warm soapy water to wash it quickly and then replace it. The steam valve is present on the inside of the lid, and to clean this, remove the shield covers. It might pop off, or you might have to unscrew it depending on the model you use. Once you wash the shield, replace it. Check the condensation cup attached to the inside of the instant pot. If it looks dirty, wash it and then replace it.

The first step is to clean the ceiling ring. It is present on the underside of the lid. So, remove the lid and inspect the silicone ring carefully. If you notice that there is any damage, deformities, or even any cracks appearing, replace it as soon as you possibly can. Use the top rack of the dishwasher to clean the silicone ring. You can also steam cleaner for removing any odors present. Once this is clean, replace it in the lead and ensure that it fits snugly.

The sixth step is to wash the inner pot, along with any other accessories present in the instant pot. This means washing the steam rack, inner pot, or any other accessories you regularly use. The steam rack, as well as the inner pot, can be safely washed in the dishwasher. However, always check the labeling present on the different accessories before you throw them all in the dishwasher. If you don't want to use the dishwasher, hand wash them regularly. Once all these parts are clean, wipe it down using a paper towel, or somebody got to make it clean. It helps remove any detergent residues and makes the surface gleam. While cleaning, don't use steel wool or any other scratchy substances since it will damage the finishing of the inner pot or aligning.

The final step is to start reassembling. Don't forget any smaller parts such as the valve shield, quick release handle, or at the sealing ring while reassembling it if you notice that the sealing ring has any funny odors, then clean it using when you go. To steam clean the instant pot, fill it with one cup of water and vinegar each along with some lemon rinds. Turn on the Instant Pot and switch on the "Steam" button for two minutes. It helps get rid of any funky food odors.

Chapter Two: Instant Pot Breakfast Recipes

Instant Pot Vegan Breakfast Recipes

Chocolate Steel Cut Oats

Serves: 2

Ingredients:

- ½ cup steel cut oats
- 1 ½ tablespoons cocoa
- 3 small bananas, mashed
- 1 ¾ cups water or nondairy milk

Directions:

1. Add all the ingredients into the instant pot and mix until well combined.
2. Close the lid. Select 'Manual' button and timer for 7 minutes. Let the pressure release naturally.
3. Stir well and serve.

Cornmeal Polenta Porridge

Serves: 2

Ingredients:

- ¼ cup coarsely ground cornmeal
- A pinch salt
- ½ teaspoon vanilla extract
- 1 cup almond milk + extra to serve
- 2 tablespoons maple syrup + extra to taste

Directions:

1. Add all the ingredients into the instant pot and stir.

2. Close the lid. Select 'Manual' button and timer for 8 minutes. Let the pressure release naturally for 3 minutes after which quick release excess pressure.
3. Pour milk and stir. Serve with maple syrup and toppings of your choice.

Toasted Granola

Serves: 8

Ingredients:

- ¼ cup maple syrup or agave nectar
- 2 tablespoons canola oil
- ½ teaspoon ground cinnamon
- ¼ cup sunflower kernels
- 2 ½ cups regular rolled oats
- ¼ cup golden raisins
- 2 tablespoons peanut butter
- 2 cups dates, pitted, chopped
- 1 tablespoon ground flaxseeds or wheat germ
- ¼ cup apple sauce

Directions:

1. Spray the inside of the instant pot with cooking spray.
2. Add applesauce, maple syrup, oil, cinnamon and peanut butter into a bowl and whisk well.
3. Add oats, sunflower kernels, applesauce and flax seeds into the instant pot and mix well.
4. Close the lid but leave a slight gap.
5. Select 'Slow cook' button and timer for 2 ½ hours. Stir 4 – 5 times during cooking (say every ½ hour).
6. When done, transfer on a sheet of foil and cool completely. Add dates and raisins and toss well.
7. Transfer into an airtight container. It can last for 5-6 days at room temperature or place in the refrigerator or freezer to last longer.
8. Serve granola with milk or yogurt and toppings of your choice.

Breakfast Quinoa with Blueberries and Bananas

Serves: 8

Ingredients:

- 2 ripe bananas, peeled, mashed

- 2 cups vanilla almond milk, unsweetened + extra to serve
- 2 cups frozen wild blueberries + extra to serve
- 1 teaspoon ground cinnamon
- 2 teaspoons vanilla extract
- 2 cups water
- 2 cups quinoa rinsed
- 2 tablespoons ground flaxseeds
- ½ teaspoon salt

Directions:

1. Add all the ingredients into the instant pot. Mix well.
2. Close the lid. Select 'Manual' and timer for 1 minute. Let the pressure release naturally for 3 minutes after which quick release excess pressure.
3. Serve with blueberries, almond milk and any other toppings of your choice.

Cranberry Apple Oatmeal

Serves: 6

Ingredients:

- 2 cups steel cut oats
- 4 Granny Smith apples, peeled, chopped
- 8 tablespoons brown sugar or to taste
- 1 cup dried cranberries
- ½ teaspoon mixed spice
- 1 teaspoon ground cinnamon
- 8 cups water

Directions:

1. Add all the ingredients to the instant pot. Mix well.
2. Close the lid. Select 'Manual' and timer for 9 minutes. Let the pressure release naturally.
3. Serve with milk and toppings of your choice such as walnuts or almonds.

French toast Casserole

Serves: 3-4

Ingredients:

- 6 ounces vegan bread, cut into cubes
- ¼ cup light brown sugar, packed
- 1 teaspoon ground cinnamon
- ½ cup vanilla almond milk
- 2 tablespoons dairy free butter, melted
- ½ teaspoon vanilla extract
- ¼ teaspoon ground nutmeg

Directions:

1. Add bread cubes into a heatproof container.
2. Add butter and sugar into a bowl. Whisk until well combined.
3. Add rest of the ingredients and mix well. Pour over the bread and mix well.
4. Pour 1 ½ cups water into the instant pot. Place a rack in the pot. Place the container over the rack.
5. Close the lid. Select 'Manual' and timer for 8 minutes. Let the pressure release naturally.
6. Serve warm.

Coconut Quinoa Breakfast Bowl

Serves: 3

Ingredients:

- ¾ cup quinoa, rinsed, soaked in water for an hour
- ¾ cup water
- 1 cup coconut milk
- ½ teaspoon ground cinnamon
- 1 teaspoon vanilla extract
- 2 tablespoons pure maple syrup
- A pinch salt

To serve: Optional

- Coconut flakes
- Coconut milk
- Any toppings of your choice

Directions:

1. Add all the ingredients into the instant pot. Mix well.
2. Close the lid. Select 'Manual' and timer for 1 minute. Let the pressure release naturally for 3 minutes after which quick release excess pressure.

3. Divide into bowls. Serve with nondairy milk of your choice.

Pumpkin Coffeecake Steel-cut Oatmeal

Serves: 3

Ingredients:

- ¾ cup steel cut oats
- 1 teaspoon ground cinnamon
- ½ teaspoon vanilla extract
- 2 ¼ cups water
- ¾ cup pumpkin puree
- ½ teaspoon allspice

For coffee cake topping:

- ¼ cup coconut sugar or any other vegan sugar
- ½ tablespoon ground cinnamon
- 2 tablespoons chopped walnuts or pecans

Directions:

1. Add all the ingredients into the instant pot and stir.
2. Close the lid. Select 'Manual' and timer for 3 minutes. Let the pressure release naturally.
3. Divide into bowls.
4. Meanwhile, add all the ingredients for topping into a bowl and mix well.
5. Divide. Scatter on top of the oatmeal and serve with some nondairy milk if desired.

Brown Rice Porridge

Serves: 2

Ingredients:

For the porridge:

- ½ teaspoon pure vanilla extract
- 1 ½ cups cooked brown rice
- 1 tablespoon raisins
- 2 tablespoons vegan coconut sugar or brown sugar
- 1 cup soy milk or almond milk, unsweetened

- ½ teaspoon ground cinnamon
- 1 tablespoon golden flaxseed meal
- A pinch salt

To serve: (optional)

- ¼ cup chopped almonds, toasted
- 2 teaspoons chia seeds
- Pomegranate arils
- 2 tablespoons shredded coconut
- Cacao nibs

Directions:

1. Add all the ingredients into the instant pot. Mix well.
2. Close the lid. Select 'Manual' and timer for 15 minutes. Let the pressure release naturally.
3. Spoon into individual bowls. Serve with any of the suggested toppings.

Banana Bread Instant Pot Steel Cut Oats

Serves: 2

Ingredients:

- 1 banana, mashed
- 1 ½ cups nondairy milk of your choice
- 2 tablespoons chopped pecans
- 1 tablespoon brown sugar
- ¼ teaspoon salt
- ½ cup steel cut oats
- 1 teaspoon ground cinnamon
- 1 tablespoon maple syrup
- ½ teaspoon vanilla extract
- Vegan butter, to serve (optional)

Directions:

1. Grease the inside of the instant pot with cooking spray.
2. Add banana, oats, milk, salt, cinnamon and vanilla and mix well.
3. Close the lid. Select 'Manual' and timer for 3 minutes. Let the pressure release naturally.
4. Add rest of the ingredients and stir. Cover and let it sit for 30 minutes.
5. Divide into bowls. Top with vegan butter if using and serve.

Breakfast Instant Pot Pie with Sausage and Beans

Serves: 3

Ingredients:

- ½ teaspoon oil
- 1 stalk celery, chopped
- 1 clove garlic, minced
- 1 teaspoon dried rosemary
- 6 – 7 ounces vegan Italian sausage, crumbled
- 2 tablespoons chopped cashews
- ½ sheet puff pastry
- 1 shallot, thinly sliced
- 1 small carrot, diced
- 2 potatoes, diced
- ½ cup dry navy beans
- 1 ½ cups vegetable stock
- Salt to taste
- Pepper to taste

Directions:

1. Press 'Sauté' button. Add oil and let it heat. Add shallot, carrot, celery, garlic, salt and pepper and stir until onions are translucent.
2. Stir in rosemary, potatoes and sausage and cook for a couple of minutes.
3. Add beans and stock and stir. Press 'Cancel' button.
4. Close the lid. Press 'Bean /Chili' button. Let the pressure release naturally.
5. Add cashews into a blender along with a little of the hot stock and blend until smooth. Pour into the pot.
6. Select 'Sauté' button and simmer until thick.
7. Meanwhile, unroll the pastry sheet and cut into circles (that can fit on the top of ramekins).
8. Place on a baking sheet.
9. Bake in a preheated oven at 375° F for about 10 minutes or golden brown and slightly puffy.
10. Spoon the sausage mixture into ramekins. Place a pastry circle on each ramekin and serve.

Sprouted Lentils Breakfast Bowl

Serves: 2 – 3

Ingredients:

- ½ tablespoon oil
- ¼ teaspoon turmeric powder
- ½ teaspoon mild chili powder
- ½ teaspoon salt
- 1 small onion, finely chopped
- ½ teaspoon grated ginger
- ½ teaspoon ground cumin
- 1 ½ cups sprouted brown lentils
- Salt to taste
- Pepper to taste
- ¼ cup water

To serve: Optional

- Chopped tomatoes
- Grated coconut
- Chopped cilantro

Directions:

1. Press 'Sauté' button. Add oil. When the oil is heated, add onion and cook until pink.
2. Add spices and salt and stir for a few seconds until aromatic.
3. Add lentils and water and stir. Press 'Cancel' button.
4. Close the lid. Press 'Manual' and timer for 1 minute. Let the pressure release naturally.
5. Divide into plates. Top with optional ingredients and serve

Miso Breakfast Oats

Serves: 4

Ingredients:

- 1 cup steel cut oats
- 2 cups water
- 2 tablespoons miso paste
- 2 teaspoons tamari
- 1 avocado, peeled, pitted, diced
- 2 cups almond milk, unsweetened
- 2 cups chopped, frozen kale
- 8 tablespoons nutritional yeast
- 2 tablespoons tahini
- 4 green onions, sliced

Directions:
1. Add oats, milk and water into the instant pot and stir.
2. Close the lid. Select 'Manual' and timer for 6 minutes. Let the pressure release naturally.
3. Add kale, tamari, miso paste, tahini and nutritional yeast and stir.
4. Press 'Sauté' button and heat thoroughly. Stir frequently.
5. Divide into bowls. Garnish with avocado and green onions and serve.

Cilantro Lime Quinoa

Serves: 3

Ingredients:
- 2 green chilies
- A handful fresh cilantro, chopped
- 1 teaspoon vegetable bouillon
- Juice of a lime
- 1 small onion, chopped
- ¾ cup quinoa
- 1 large clove garlic minced
- Salt to taste
- Pepper to taste
- ¾ cup water

Directions:
1. Add green chili, cilantro and onions into a blender and blend until smooth.
2. Pour into the instant pot. Add rest of the ingredients except lime juice and mix well.
3. Close the lid. Select 'Manual' and timer for 5 minutes. Let the pressure release naturally.
4. Fluff with a fork. Add lime juice and stir.
5.

Japanese Breakfast Sweet Potatoes

Serves: 4

Ingredients:
- 4 sweet potatoes, cubed
- Zest of ½ lemon, grated
- 4 – 6 thin lemon slices, deseeded
- 1 tablespoon chopped fresh herbs of your choice

- Sumac to taste
- 2 tablespoons olive oil

Directions:

1. Add ½ cup water into the instant pot. Place steamer basket in the pot. Place sweet potato cubes in the steamer basket.
2. Close the lid. Select 'Manual' and timer for 10 minutes. Quick release excess pressure.
3. Remove the steamer basket and discard the water from the instant pot. Wipe the pot dry.
4. Press 'Sauté' button. Add oil. When the oil is heated, add lemon slices and fresh herbs and stir frequently until slightly crisp on the lemon rinds.
5. Add sweet potatoes and cook until brown. Add more oil if required. Press 'Cancel' button.
6. Transfer into a bowl. Sprinkle salt, sumac and some more herbs and toss well.

Low Carb Breakfast Recipes

Omelet Bites

Serves: 3

Ingredients:

- 2 eggs, beaten
- ¼ cup grated cheddar cheese
- ¼ cup crumbled cottage cheese
- 1 green onion, thinly sliced
- 4 mushrooms, diced
- ½ green bell pepper, diced
- Seasoned salt to taste
- Pepper to taste
- Salt to taste
- ¼ teaspoon ground mustard
- ¼ teaspoon garlic powder
- 1 slice deli ham, diced small
- A dash hot sauce

Directions:

1. Add cottage cheese and cheddar cheese into the bowl of eggs and whisk well.
2. Add rest of the ingredients and mix well.
3. Divide into a greased heatproof container.
4. Pour 1 ½ cups water into the instant pot. Place a rack in it. Place container on the rack.

5. Close the lid. Select 'Manual' and timer for 8 minutes. Let the pressure release naturally for 10 minutes after which quick release excess pressure.
6. Remove the container and cool completely. Cut into pieces and serve.

Mediterranean Breakfast Casserole

Serves: 4

Ingredients:

- 2 large egg whites
- 4 large eggs
- 2 tablespoons almond milk
- ½ tablespoon chopped fresh oregano
- 1 Roma tomato, chopped
- 2 canned artichoke hearts, chopped
- 2 ounces fresh baby spinach
- 1/3 cup sliced mushrooms
- ¼ cup finely chopped green onions
- ½ teaspoon minced garlic
- 1/8 teaspoon garlic powder
- ½ teaspoon salt or to taste
- ½ teaspoon pepper or to taste
- 2 tablespoons crumbled feta cheese
- 1 tablespoon freshly grated parmesan cheese

Directions:

1. Add eggs, whites, milk, Parmesan cheese, oregano, garlic powder, salt and pepper into a large bowl. Whisk well. Add green onion, garlic, tomatoes, mushrooms and spinach. Fold gently and pour into a heatproof container. Sprinkle feta cheese over it.
2. Pour 1 ½ cups water into the instant pot. Place a steamer rack in the pot and the container on the rack.
3. Close the lid. Select 'Manual' button and timer for 12 minutes. Let the pressure release naturally. Do not open the lid for 10 minutes. Let it cool on the countertop for 10 minutes.
4. Slice into wedges and serve.

Healthy Egg Muffins

: Serves: 6

Ingredients

- 2 large egg whites
- 2 eggs
- ½ cup chopped green bell pepper
- ½ cup chopped red bell pepper
- ½ cup diced onion
- ½ cup sliced mushrooms
- 1 cup chopped baby spinach
- Salt to taste
- Pepper to taste
- ½ tablespoon olive oil
- 1 clove garlic, peeled, minced
- Hot sauce to drizzle (optional)

Directions:

1. Add eggs, whites, salt and pepper into a bowl and whisk well.
2. Add rest of the ingredients and whisk well.
3. Grease 6 muffin cups with olive oil. Divide and pour the egg mixture into 6 ramekins.
4. Pour 1 ½ cups water into the instant pot. Place steamer rack in.
5. Close the lid. Select 'Manual' button and timer f0r 8 minutes. Let the pressure release naturally.
6. Serve hot.

Broccoli Ham and Pepper Frittata

Serves: 8

Ingredients:

- 16 ounces ham, cubed
- 4 cups frozen broccoli
- 2 cups half and half
- 1 teaspoon salt or to taste
- 1 cup chopped red bell pepper
- 1 cup chopped yellow bell pepper

- 8 eggs
- 2 cups shredded cheddar cheese
- 2-3 teaspoons pepper or to taste
- Cooking spray

Directions:

1. Grease a heatproof container generously with cooking spray.
2. Spread bell peppers on the bottom of the pan. Spread ham followed by broccoli.
3. Add eggs, cream, salt and pepper into a bowl and whisk well. Add cheese and mix well.
4. Pour over the broccoli. Do not stir. Cover the dish with aluminum foil.
5. Pour 2 cups water into the instant pot. Place a steamer rack in the pot and container on the rack.
6. Close the lid. Press 'Manual' button and timer for 20 minutes.
7. Let the pressure release naturally for 10 minutes after which quick release excess pressure.
8. Let it remain covered for 10 minutes.
9. Run a knife around the edges of the frittata. Invert on to a plate. Broil for a couple of minutes if desired.
10. Slice into wedges and serve.

Egg Cheese Bake

Serves: 6

Ingredients:

- 6 eggs
- ¾ cup shredded Sharp cheddar cheese
- Salt to taste
- Pepper to taste
- 1 ½ cups mixed, chopped vegetables of your choice
- 1/3 cup half and half
- A handful cilantro, chopped
- ½ cup shredded cheese, to top

Directions:

1. Whisk together all the ingredients in a bowl.

2. Cover the container with foil.
3. Pour 1 ½ cups water into the instant pot. Place a steamer rack in the pot.
4. Place the container over the rack.
5. Close the lid. Press 'Manual' button and timer for 5 minutes.
6. Let the container remain in the pot for 10 minutes.
7. Sprinkle cheese on top. Broil for 2-3 minutes.
8. Cut into 6 wedges and serve.

Chili and Cheese Frittata

Serves: 8

Ingredients:

- 8 eggs, whisked
- 20 ounces canned green chilies, drained, chopped
- 1 teaspoon ground cumin
- ½ cup fresh cilantro, chopped
- 2 cups half and half
- 1 teaspoon salt or to taste
- 2 cups shredded, Mexican blend cheese, divided

Directions:

1. Add half and half, cumin, salt and 1 cup cheese into the bowl of eggs. Mix until well combined.
2. Pour into a heatproof bowl. Cover the bowl with foil.
3. Pour 1 ½ cups water into the instant pot. Place a steamer rack in it.
4. Place the bowl over the rack.
5. Close the lid. Select 'Manual' button and set timer for 20 minutes.
6. When the timer goes off, quick release excess pressure.
7. Sprinkle remaining cheese on top. Broil for 5 minutes and serve.
8. Cut into 8 wedges and serve.

Breakfast Casserole

Serves: 3

Ingredients:

- 1 tablespoon coconut oil
- 1 teaspoon minced garlic
- 4 eggs
- ¾ cup cooked breakfast sausages
- 2/3 cup sliced leeks
- ½ cup kale, chopped, discard hard rib and stems
- 1/3 cup grated sweet potato

Directions:

1. Press 'Sauté' button. Add oil. When oil melts, add garlic, kale and leeks and sauté until kale wilts. Turn off the heat.
2. Remove the vegetables and place on a plate. Wipe the pot clean.
3. Whisk eggs in a bowl. Add sweet potato, sausage and the sautéed vegetables and mix well.
4. Transfer into a heatproof bowl.
5. Pour 1 ½ cups water into the instant pot. Place a rack or trivet in it.
6. Place the heatproof container over the rack.
7. Close the lid. Select 'Manual' button and timer for 25 minutes.
8. When the timer goes off, quick release excess pressure. Remove container from the pot and let it rest for 10 minutes. Loosen the edges with a knife. Invert onto a plate.
9. Cut into equal wedges and serve.

Omelet Casserole

Serves: 2 – 3

Ingredients:

- 1 cup + 2 tablespoons grated mozzarella cheese + extra to top
- ¼ green bell pepper, diced
- 3 eggs
- 1 tablespoon chopped parsley, to garnish
- ½ cup diced mushrooms
- ½ cup roasted potatoes or leftover potatoes
- 2 tablespoons milk or cream (optional)

Directions:

1. Take a small casserole dish and grease with oil. Sprinkle 2 tablespoons mozzarella cheese on the bottom of the dish.
2. Scatter the vegetables over the cheese in the dish.

3. Add eggs into a bowl and whisk well. Add milk and whisk well. Add 1 cup cheese and whisk well.
4. Pour over the vegetables.
5. Pour 1 cup water into the instant pot. Place a rack in the pot. Place the casserole dish over the rack.
6. Close the lid. Select 'Manual' button and timer for 10 minutes. Let the pressure release naturally.
7. Garnish with cheese and parsley and serve.

Blueberry Muffins

Serves: 12

Ingredients:

For dry ingredients:

- 2/3 cup coconut flour
- 9 tablespoons erythritol or swerve
- ½ teaspoon baking soda
- 2 teaspoons baking powder
- ¼ teaspoon salt
- 3 tablespoons golden flaxseed meal

For wet ingredients:

- 2/3 cup unsweetened almond milk
- 3 tablespoons melted butter
- 4 large eggs, beaten
- 2 teaspoons vanilla extract

Other ingredients:

- 2/3 cup fresh blueberries

Directions:
1. Add all the dry ingredients into a large mixing bowl and stir well.
2. Add all the wet ingredients into another bowl and whisk well. Pour the wet ingredients into the bowl of dry ingredients and mix until smooth.
3. Add blueberries and fold gently.
4. Divide the batter into 12 muffin cups.
5. Pour 1 ½ cups water into the instant pot. Place a steamer rack in the pot. Place a sheet of foil on the rack. Place the muffin cups on the rack (place as many as that can fit in and cook the remaining in batches). Place another sheet of foil on top of the muffin cups.

6. Close the lid. Select 'Manual' button and timer for 20 minutes. Let the pressure release naturally for 10 minutes after which quick release excess pressure.
7. Remove the muffin cups and let it cool for a few minutes. Run a knife around the edges of the muffins to loosen them. Invert onto a plate and serve.
8. Leftovers can be stored in an airtight container in the refrigerator. It can last for 5 – 6 days.
9.

Crustless Meaty Quiche

Serves: 12

Ingredients:

- 12 large eggs
- Salt to taste
- Pepper to taste
- 8 slices bacon, cooked, crumbled
- 1 cup diced ham
- 2 cups ground sausage, cooked
- 1 cup milk
- 2 cups cheese, shredded

Directions:

1. Add eggs, milk, salt and pepper into a bowl and whisk well.
2. Add meat, cheese, and green onions and place in a greased heatproof container.
3. Pour egg mixture over it and stir.
4. Pour 1 ½ cups water into the instant pot. Place a rack or trivet in it.
5. Place the container on the rack.
6. Close the lid. Select 'Manual' button and timer for 20 minutes. Let the pressure release naturally for 10 minutes after which quick release excess pressure.
7. Garnish with some extra cheese on top if desired and serve.

Omelet Quiche

Serves: 6

Ingredients:

- 12 large eggs
- Himalayan pink salt to taste
- 2 green onions, thinly sliced
- 12-14 ounces Canadian bacon, chopped

- 1 cup half and half
- 1 ½ cups chopped, mixed color bell peppers
- Pepper to taste
- 1 ½ cups shredded cheese + extra (optional) to garnish

Directions:

1. Whisk the eggs well. Add half and half, salt and pepper and whisk well.
2. Grease a soufflé dish or any heatproof container with a little butter or oil.
3. Add bacon, bell pepper, cheese and whites of the green onions into the dish and toss well.
4. Pour egg mixture over it and stir. Cover the dish loosely with aluminum foil.
5. Pour 1 ½ cups water in the inner pot of the instant pot. Place a trivet in it.
6. Place the container on the trivet.
7. Close the lid. Select 'Manual' and timer for 30 minutes.
8. Let the pressure release naturally for 10 minutes after which quick release excess pressure.
9. Sprinkle some cheese on top if using and broil for 1 – 2 minutes or until light golden brown.
10. Sprinkle greens of the green onions on top. Cut into wedges and serve.

Scotch Eggs

Serves: 2

Ingredients:

- 2 large eggs
- ½ tablespoon olive oil
- ½ pound country style ground sausage

Directions:

1. Pour 1 cup water into the instant pot. Place a trivet or steamer rack in it.
2. Place the eggs on the trivet.
3. Close the lid. Select 'Manual' and timer for 6 minutes.
4. Quick release the excess pressure.
5. Remove eggs and place in a bowl of cold water for a few minutes. Remove the eggs and peel.
6. Divide the sausage into 2 equal portions and shape into a flat round. Place an egg in the center of one portion and enclose the egg with the sausage from all sides. Repeat with the other egg and sausage portion.
7. Select 'Sauté' button. Add oil to the instant pot. When oil is heated, place the Scotch eggs and cook until brown from all sides. Remove from the cooker and set aside. Press 'Cancel' button.

8. Pour a cup of water in the pot. Place a trivet or steamer rack in it and place the Scotch eggs on it.
9. Close the lid. Select 'Manual' and timer for 6 minutes.
10. Quick release the excess pressure.
11. Cut into 2 halves. Season with salt and pepper and serve.

Low Carb Egg Benedict

Serves: 4

Ingredients:

For muffins:

- 4 tablespoons melted butter
- 4 tablespoons almond meal
- 1 teaspoon baking powder
- 8 egg whites

For poached eggs:

- 1 cup water
- 4 eggs

For Hollandaise sauce:

- 8 egg yolks
- Salt to taste
- 2 tablespoons lemon juice
- 1 cup unsalted butter, melted and very hot

Other ingredients:

- 16 spinach leaves
- 4 – 8 slices bacon or ham

Directions:

1. For muffins: Add butter, almond flour and baking powder into a mixing bowl and mix well.
2. Add egg whites and mix until smooth batter is formed.
3. Grease 6 muffin cups with olive oil. Divide and pour the egg mixture into the muffin cups.
4. Pour 1 ½ cups water into the instant pot. Place steamer rack in. Place the muffin cups on the rack.

5. Close the lid. Select 'Manual' button and timer f0r 8 minutes. Let the pressure release naturally.
6. To poach eggs: Retain only a cup of water in the instant pot and discard the remaining water.
7. Place a trivet or rack in the pot.
8. Take 4 ramekins and grease with a little oil or butter. Crack an egg into each ramekin. Place the ramekins on the rack.
9. Close the lid. Select 'Manual' and timer for 1 - 2 minutes depending on how you like the eggs cooked.
10. Quick release the excess pressure.
11. Remove the eggs carefully from the ramekins with a spoon.
12. To make hollandaise sauce: Add yolks, lemon juice and salt into a blender and blend until smooth.
13. Add butter and blend until smooth.
14. To assemble: Split the muffins. Toast the muffins halves to the desired crispiness. Place on a serving platter.
15. Place 4 spinach leaves on each of the bottom halves of the muffins. Layer with bacon slices followed by a poached egg. Spoon some hollandaise sauce on top. Cover with the top half of the muffins and serve.

Coconut Low Carb Porridge

Serves: 3

Ingredients:

- ½ cup unsweetened shredded coconut
- 1 1/3 cups water
- 2 tablespoons whole psyllium husks
- ¼ teaspoon ground cinnamon
- 10 drops monk fruit liquid sweetener or to taste
- 15 drops liquid stevia or to taste
- 1 cup coconut milk
- 2 tablespoons coconut flour
- ½ teaspoon vanilla extract
- 1/8 teaspoon ground nutmeg

Directions:

1. Press 'Sauté' button. Add coconut and stir frequently until golden brown. Keep a watch as it can get burnt very easily.
2. Pour water and coconut milk and mix well.
3. Close the lid. Select 'Manual' and timer for 0 minute. Let the pressure release naturally for 8 minutes after which quick release excess pressure.

4. Uncover and add rest of the ingredients. Mix well and serve in bowls with low carb toppings of your choice.

Banana Nut Bread

Serves: 5

Ingredients:

- 1 cup low-carb baking mix
- 1 tablespoon butter, at room temperature
- 3 tablespoons unsweetened apple sauce
- 2 tablespoons chopped nuts
- ¼ teaspoon salt
- ½ cup mashed, overripe banana
- 1 egg
- 2 tablespoons powdered stevia
- ¾ teaspoon baking soda

Directions:

1. Add butter, stevia, applesauce and eggs into a bowl. Beat with an electric hand mixer until creamy. Mix in the banana.
2. Add baking mix, salt, and baking soda into another bowl and stir until well combined. Add into the bowl of butter and beat until well incorporated.
3. Add nuts and fold gently.
4. Pour into a greased heatproof container. Cover the container with foil.
5. Pour 1 ½ cups water into the instant pot. Place a rack or trivet in it.
6. Place the container on the trivet. Close the lid. Select 'Manual' and timer for 30 minutes.
7. Let the pressure release naturally. Remove the container from the instant pot and cool completely.
8. Cut into 5 slices and serve.

Chapter Three: Instant Pot Soup Recipes

Cheesy Cauliflower Soup

Serves: 8

Ingredients:

- 4 – 6 tablespoons butter
- 12 cups vegetable broth
- 2 heaping cups shredded cheese
- 2 onions, chopped
- 2 heads cauliflower, cut into florets (about 12 cups)
- 2 tablespoons truffle oil (optional but recommended)
- Salt to taste
- Pepper to taste

Directions:

1. Press 'Sauté' button. Add butter. When butter melts, add onions and cook until golden brown.
2. Add broth and cauliflower and stir.
3. Close the lid. Select 'Soup' button and timer for 20 minutes. Quick release excess pressure.
4. Blend with an immersion blender until smooth. Stir in the cheese. When cheese melts, add truffle oil if using and stir.
5. Ladle into soup bowls and serve with croutons or some more cheese if desired.

Black Bean Soup

Serves: 5

Ingredients:

- 2 cups chicken broth
- ½ can (from a 14.4 ounces can) black beans, drained, rinsed
- ½ can (from a 14.4 ounces can) diced tomatoes
- ½ can (from a 14.5 ounces can) corn, drained, rinsed
- ½ can (from a 14.4 ounces can) fat-free refried beans
- Salt to taste
- Pepper to taste

Directions:

1. Add all the ingredients into the instant pot and mix well.
2. Close the lid. Select 'Manual' and timer for 8 minutes. Quick release excess pressure.
3. Ladle into soup bowls and serve with avocado and sour cream if desired.

Beef and Macaroni Soup

Serves: 4

Ingredients:

- ½ pound extra lean ground beef
- ½ cup frozen spinach
- ½ cup chopped red bell pepper
- ¾ cup whole grain elbow macaroni, uncooked
- 1 clove garlic, minced
- 1 medium onion, chopped
- 1 ½ cups low-sodium beef broth
- 13 ounces canned tomato pasta sauce
- Salt to taste
- Pepper to taste
- ½ teaspoon dried oregano
- ½ tablespoon dried basil
- ¼ teaspoon crushed red pepper flakes
- 1 can (14.4 ounces) diced tomatoes

Directions:

1. Press 'Sauté' button. Add beef and sauté until brown. Add garlic and sauté for a couple of minutes until aromatic. Press 'Cancel' button.
2. Add rest of the ingredients into the pot and mix well.
3. Close the lid. Select 'Soup' button and timer for 20 minutes.

4. Let the pressure release naturally.
5. Ladle into soup bowls and serve.

Creamy Chicken and Mushroom Soup

Serves: 8

Ingredients:

- 4 cup chopped mushrooms
- 2 onions, thinly sliced
- 2 pounds chicken breast, skinless, chopped into large chunks
- 2 yellow squash, chopped
- 5 cups chicken stock
- 1 tablespoon Italian seasoning

To serve:

- Heavy whipping cream (optional)

Directions

1. Add all the ingredients to the instant pot and stir.
2. Close the lid. Select 'Poultry' button. Let the pressure release naturally for 10 minutes after which quick release excess pressure.
3. Remove chicken with a slotted spoon and place on your cutting board. When cool enough to handle, shred with a pair of forks and add it back into the pot. Mix well.
4. Ladle into soup bowls. Drizzle some heavy cream if using and stir.

Butternut Squash Soup

Serves: 4

Ingredients:

- ½ pound peeled, butternut squash cubes
- 1 large carrot, peeled, chopped into chunks
- 1 small onion, chopped
- 1 small Granny Smith apple, peeled, cored, sliced
- 1 bay leaf
- ½ teaspoon pepper or to taste
- ½ teaspoon salt or to taste
- 7 ounces canned coconut milk
- ¼ teaspoon dried ground sage
- 2 cups vegetable broth

To serve: Optional

- Croutons
- Crusty bread

Directions:

1. Add onion, squash, carrot, apple, bay leaf and vegetable broth into the instant pot and stir.
2. Close the lid. Select 'Manual' button and timer for 12 minutes. Let the pressure release naturally.
3. Discard bay leaf. Blend with an immersion blender until smooth.
4. Add salt, pepper, sage and coconut milk. Heat if desired.

5. Ladle into soup bowls and serve with suggested serving options.

Chicken "Noodle" Soup

Serves: 8

Ingredients:

- 4 tablespoons coconut oil
- 2 cups diced celery
- 1 ½ cups chopped greens of green onions
- 2 cups diced carrots
- 2 pounds skinless, boneless chicken thighs
- Salt to taste
- Pepper to taste
- 12 cups chicken stock
- 1 teaspoon dried oregano
- 1 teaspoon dried basil
- 4 cups daikon noodles

Directions:

1. Make noodles of daikon using a spiralizer or julienne peeler. Measure out 4 cups of the noodles and set aside.
2. Press 'Sauté' button. Add oil. When the oil is heated, add chicken and sauté until chicken is tender.
3. Remove with a slotted spoon and place on your cutting board. When cool enough to handle, shred with a pair of forks. Add it back into the pot.
4. Add green onions, carrots, and celery and sauté for a couple of minutes.
5. Add rest of the ingredients except daikon noodles.
6. Close the lid. Press 'Soup' button and timer for 15 minutes.
7. Let the pressure release naturally.
8. Add daikon noodles and stir.
9. Ladle into soup bowls and serve.

Lasagna Soup (Beef/ Vegetarian)

Serves: 4

Ingredients:

- ¾ pound lean ground beef or sausage / vegetarian sausage crumble for a vegetarian soup
- 2 inches sprig rosemary
- 1 large onion, chopped
- 2 handfuls spinach, chopped
- 2 ½ cups beef broth / vegetable broth for a vegetarian soup
- ½ can (from a 28 ounces can) diced tomatoes
- ½ can (from a 14 ounces can) tomato sauce
- 2 ounces mushrooms, sliced
- 6 cloves garlic, minced
- ½ teaspoon dried oregano
- ½ teaspoon dried basil
- Red pepper flakes to taste
- 1 bay leaf
- Salt to taste
- Pepper to taste
- 1 ½ cups water
- 4 – 5 lasagna noodles, broken
- ½ cup grated parmesan cheese + extra to garnish
- ½ cup cottage cheese or ricotta
- ½ cup grated mozzarella cheese
- A handful fresh parsley or basil, chopped, to garnish

Directions:

1. Press 'Sauté' button. When the pot heats, add bay leaf, beef and rosemary and cook until the meat is not pink anymore. Discard cooked fat if desired.
2. Add onion, salt, herbs and seasonings and cook until onion is slightly soft.
3. Stir in the garlic and mushrooms. Add tomato sauce, tomatoes and broth and mix well. Press 'Cancel' button.
4. Stir in the pasta.
5. Close the lid. Select 'Manual' and timer for 6 minutes. Quick release excess pressure.
6. Stir in spinach and all the cheeses.
7. Ladle into soup bowls. Garnish with parmesan and parsley and serve

Carnitas Soup

Serves: 8

Ingredients:

For soup:

- 3 cups chicken stock
- 8 cups Carnitas
- 4 teaspoons ground cumin
- 2 pounds Yukon gold potatoes, diced
- 4 cups salsa verde
- Salt to taste
- Pepper to taste

Optional toppings:

- 2 handfuls arugula
- 1 large avocado, peeled, pitted, chopped
- Grated cheese
- Jalapeño slices

Directions:

1. Add all the ingredients for soup into the instant pot and stir.
2. Close the lid. Select 'Manual' and timer for 8 minutes. Quick release excess pressure.
3. Ladle into soup bowls and serve with any of the optional toppings if desired.

Chapter Four: Instant Pot Vegan Recipes

Tempeh, Potato and Kale Bowl

Serves: 2

Ingredients:

For potato layer:

- 14 ounces new or baby potatoes, quartered

For tempeh layer:

- 1 tablespoon maple syrup
- ½ teaspoon hot sauce
- 2 teaspoons water
- 1 teaspoon soy sauce
- 4 ounces tempeh, cubed

For kale layer:

- 2 cups chopped kale
- 2 teaspoons water
- 1 tablespoon nutritional yeast
- ½ teaspoon minced garlic

For potato seasoning:

- Salt to taste
- Pepper to taste
- ½ teaspoon smoked paprika

Directions:

1. To make potato layer: Pour 1 ½ cups water into the instant pot. Place the steamer rack in it. Place potatoes over the rack.
2. To make tempeh layer. Place all the ingredients for tempeh layer into a short heatproof pan and toss well. Cover the pan with foil. Place the pan over the potatoes.
3. To make kale layer: Add all the ingredients for kale layer into a short heatproof pan and mix well. Cover the pan with foil and place over the other heatproof bowl.
4. Close the lid. Select 'Manual' and timer for 5 minutes. Let the pressure release naturally.
5. Mix together all the ingredients for potato seasoning into a bowl. Transfer the potatoes into a bowl. Sprinkle seasoning over the potatoes.
6. Divide into 2 bowls. Divide the tempeh among the bowls. Finally top with equal quantities of kale in each bowl and serve.

Vegan Quinoa Burrito Bowls

Serves: 2

Ingredients:

- ½ teaspoon extra-virgin olive oil
- ½ bell pepper, diced
- 1 small onion, diced
- Salt to taste
- ½ cup quinoa, rinsed
- ½ cup water
- ½ cup prepared salsa
- ¾ cup cooked or canned black beans

Optional toppings:

- 2 lettuce leaves, shredded
- 1 large avocado, peeled, pitted, chopped
- Grated cheese
- Guacamole
- Salsa
- Cilantro etc.

Directions:

1. Select 'Sauté' button. Add oil to the instant pot. When oil is heated, add onion and bell pepper and cook until slightly tender.
2. Stir in the cumin and salt. Stir for a few seconds until aromatic.
3. Add rest of the ingredients and stir.
4. Close the lid. Select 'Rice' button. Fluff with a fork.
5. Divide into bowls. Place any of optional toppings over the quinoa and serve.

Vegetable and Tofu Curry

Serves: 8

Ingredients:

- 2 small egg plants, chopped
- 32 ounces extra firm tofu, drained, pressed of excess moisture, cubed
- 2 cups vegetable broth
- 2 tablespoons minced fresh ginger
- Salt to taste
- 2 medium onions, chopped
- 1 ½ cups frozen peas
- 3 cups sliced bell pepper of any color
- 6-8 tablespoons Thai green or red curry paste
- 2 cans (14.5 ounces each) coconut milk
- 2 tablespoons coconut sugar or to taste
- 1 teaspoon turmeric powder
- 1 tablespoon oil

To serve: Optional

- Hot cooked brown rice
- Hot cooked quinoa

Directions:

1. Press 'Sauté' button. Add oil. When the oil is heated, tofu and cook until golden brown all over. Remove onto a plate and set aside.
2. Add more oil if required. Add onion and sauté until translucent. Add turmeric and ginger and stir for a few seconds until aromatic. Press 'Cancel' button.
3. Add rest of the ingredients and mix well.
4. Close the lid. Select 'Manual' button and set the timer for 8 minutes. Quick release excess pressure.
5. Press 'Sauté' button. Add tofu and stir. Simmer for a few minutes.

6. When done, stir and serve over cooked quinoa or brown rice.

Persian Chickpea Stew

Serves: 8

Ingredients

- 1 cup dried chickpeas, rinsed, soaked in water for 7 – 8 hours, drained
- 4 large waxy potatoes, peeled, cut into bite size cubes
- 2 onions, chopped
- 3 – 4 large carrots, cut into bite size cubes
- 2 teaspoons cumin seeds
- 2 teaspoons fennel seeds
- 1 – 2 teaspoons chili powder
- 2 teaspoons ground coriander
- 2 teaspoons dried lime powder
- 2 teaspoons turmeric powder
- 2 cans (14 ounces each) chopped tomatoes
- 2 – 4 tablespoons harissa or to taste
- 2 tablespoons tomato puree
- 2 vegetable stock cubes, crumbled
- 2 cups water
- Cooking spray
- A handful fresh cilantro or parsley, chopped, to garnish

Directions:

1. Spray generously, the inside of the instant pot with cooking spray.
2. Press 'Sauté' button. Add onion and sauté until translucent.
3. Stir in the spices and cook for a few seconds until aromatic.
4. Add tomato puree and tomatoes and mix well. Add water and vegetable stock cubes. Mix well.
5. Add chickpeas, potatoes and carrots and mix well.
6. Close the lid. Select 'Manual' button and set the timer for 12 minutes. Let the pressure release naturally.
7. Add harissa and stir. Taste and adjust the seasoning if required.
8. Garnish with cilantro and serve.

Vegan Spaghetti

Serves: 2 – 3

Ingredients:

- 1 can (14 ounces) crushed, fire roasted tomatoes
- ½ tablespoon balsamic vinegar
- ½ teaspoon dried oregano
- 1 cup tightly packed, baby spinach leaves
- 4 ounces spaghetti, halved
- Nutritional yeast to garnish
- 1 cup water
- 1 tablespoon olive oil
- 1 teaspoon garlic powder
- ½ teaspoon salt or to taste
- Pepper to taste
- 4 fresh basil leaves, torn

Directions:

1. Add all the ingredients except spaghetti into a bowl and mix well.
2. Spread some sauce mixture on the bottom of the instant pot. Place spaghetti in the pot and spread it all over. Spread remaining sauce mixture over the spaghetti.
3. Select 'Manual' button and timer for 6 minutes. Quick release excess pressure. Stir and cool for 5 minutes.
4. Divide into bowls and serve.

Cauliflower Bolognese with Zucchini Noodles

Serves: 2

Ingredients:

- 1 medium head cauliflower, broken into florets
- 2 cloves garlic, minced
- ½ cup diced onions
- ¾ teaspoon dried basil
- Red pepper flakes to taste

- 1 teaspoon dried oregano flakes
- ¼ cup vegetable broth
- 1 ½ cans (14 ounce each) diced tomatoes
- Salt to taste
- Pepper to taste

For the noodles:

- 4 medium zucchini

Directions:

1. Add all the ingredients except zucchini to the instant pot.
2. Close the lid. Select 'Manual' button and set the timer for 12 minutes. Let the pressure release naturally.
3. Meanwhile, make noodles of the zucchini using a spiralizer using blade A or a julienne peeler.
4. Mash the cauliflower with a potato masher.
5. Divide the noodles into 4 bowls. Serve cauliflower Bolognese over the noodles.

Pumpkin Walnut Chili

Serves: 4 – 6

Ingredients:

For chili:

- ½ can (from a 28 ounces can) fire roasted tomatoes
- 2 cloves garlic, minced
- 1 – 2 chipotle peppers, chopped
- ½ cup red lentils, rinsed
- 1 small onion, minced
- 1 poblano pepper, chopped
- 1 cup chopped walnuts
- ½ cup bulgur
- ½ cup red lentils
- 1 tablespoon chili powder
- ½ tablespoon salt or to taste
- ½ tablespoon smoked paprika
- 3 cups water or vegetable broth

Other ingredients:

- 1 – 1 ½ cans (14.5 ounces each) black beans, rinsed, drained
- ½ can (from a 14 ounces can) pumpkin puree
- Toppings of your choice

Directions:

1. Add all the ingredients for chili into the instant pot and stir.
2. Close the lid. Press Soup' button and timer for 15 minutes. Let the pressure release naturally.
3. Add pumpkin puree and black beans and stir.
4. Press 'Sauté' button. Add black beans and pumpkin puree and stir. Heat thoroughly.
5. Ladle into soup bowls. Serve with toppings of your choice.

Chapter Five: Instant Pot Poultry Recipes

Chicken Burrito Bowls

Serves: 2

Ingredients:

- ½ pound skinless, boneless, chicken breasts, cut into 1 inch chunks
- ½ cup chicken broth
- ½ can (from a 15 ounces can) black beans, drained, rinsed
- ½ can (from a 4.5 ounces can) chopped green chilies
- ½ cup shredded Mexican blend cheese
- 1 teaspoon taco seasoning or to taste
- ½ can (from a 15 ounces can) corn kernels, drained, rinsed
- ½ cup salsa
- ½ cup long grain rice
- A handful fresh cilantro leaves, chopped

Directions:

1. Place chicken in the instant pot. Sprinkle taco seasoning over the chicken. Pour broth over it.
2. Add rest of the ingredients except cheese and cilantro and mix well.
3. Close the lid. Select 'Manual' button and set the timer for 10 minutes. Let the pressure release naturally.
4. Add cheese and stir. Garnish with cilantro and serve.
5.

Chicken Pot Pie

Serves: 2

Ingredients:

- ½ cup chicken broth
- ½ cup chopped baby carrots
- 3 fresh chicken tenders
- Pepper to taste
- Salt to taste
- ¼ cup milk
- 3 small potatoes, peeled, cut into cubes
- 1 small onion, minced
- ¼ cup frozen peas (do not thaw)

For butter and flour paste:

- ½ tablespoon flour
- ½ tablespoon butter, melted

Directions:
1. Add all the ingredients except milk and peas into the instant pot and stir.
2. Close the lid. Select 'Manual' button and set the timer for 3 minutes. Let the pressure release naturally for 6 minutes after which quick release excess pressure.
3. Remove chicken with a slotted spoon and place on a plate. When cool enough to handle, shred with a pair of forks.
4. Stir in the peas.
5. Now stir in the milk.
6. Whisk together butter and flour in a bowl.
7. Press 'Sauté' button. When the mixture begins to simmer, add butter mixture and stir constantly until thick.
8. Add shredded chicken and mix well.
9. Serve hot.

Hawaiian Barbeque Chicken

Serves: 2

Ingredients:

- 2 large chicken breasts, skinless, fresh or frozen
- ½ cup barbeque sauce, divided
- 1 cup canned pineapples chunks with some juice from the can
- Salt to taste
- Pepper to taste
- 1 clove garlic, peeled, minced
- ½ tablespoon red chili flakes or to taste
- 1 tablespoon cornstarch mixed with 1 tablespoon water
- ½ tablespoon vegetable oil

To serve:

- Hot cooked rice
- 1 green onion, thinly sliced

Directions:
1. Press 'Sauté' button. Add oil. When the oil is heated, add chicken and cook for a couple of minutes.
2. Add garlic and cook for a few seconds until aromatic. Press 'Cancel' button.
3. Add ¼ cup BBQ sauce and pineapple juice and mix well. Add salt, pepper and red chili flakes and stir.
4. Close the lid. Select 'Manual' button and set the timer for 3 minutes. Quick release excess pressure.

5. Uncover and add cornstarch mixture.
6. Press 'Sauté' button. Add pineapple chunks and ¼ cup BBQ sauce and stir constantly until thick.
7. Garnish with green onions and serve over rice.
8.

Salsa Lime Chicken

Serves: 3

Ingredients:

- 1 ½ pounds chicken breasts, boneless, cut into chunks
- 8 ounces salsa
- Juice of a lime
- Paprika to taste
- Salt to taste

Directions:

1. Add all the ingredients to the instant pot and stir.
2. Close lid. Select 'Poultry' button and timer for 25 minutes. Quick release excess pressure.
3. Mix well and serve.

Teriyaki Chicken and Rice

Serves: 2

Ingredients:

- 1 ¼ cups chicken broth
- 1 ½ tablespoons low-sodium soy sauce
- ½ tablespoon white vinegar
- ½ teaspoon minced ginger
- ¾ cup long grain brown rice
- 1 cup broccoli
- ½ red bell pepper, chopped
- 2 tablespoons hoisin sauce
- 1 tablespoon honey
- 1 teaspoon minced garlic
- A pinch red pepper flakes
- 1 chicken breast, skinless, boneless
- ½ cup frozen peas, thawed
- ½ cup frozen carrot, thawed
- 1 tsp black and white sesame seeds

Directions:

1. Add all the ingredients except chicken, broccoli, peas and carrots into the instant pot and stir.
2. Add rice and mix well. Place chicken over the rice.
3. Close the lid. Press 'Rice' button.
4. Add peas, broccoli and carrots into a microwave safe bowl. Cook on high for a couple of minutes until hot.
5. Remove chicken and place on your cutting board. Cut into slices.
6. Add carrot and peas into the instant pot and stir into the rice.
7. Divide into plates. Place chicken slices on top, garnish with sesame seeds and serve.

Chili Lime Chicken

Serves: 2

Ingredients:

- 1 pound chicken breasts, skinless, boneless, cut into 2 halves, horizontally, if more than an inch in thickness
- ¾ teaspoon chili powder
- 1 teaspoon onion powder
- 3 cloves garlic, minced
- ½ teaspoon cumin powder
- Juice of 1 lime
- ¼ teaspoon liquid smoke
- Pepper to taste
- Salt to taste

Directions:

1. Add all the ingredients except chicken into a bowl and mix well. Rub this mixture all over the chicken.
2. Place the chicken in the instant pot.
3. Close the lid. Select 'Manual' button and timer for 6 minutes. Let the pressure release naturally for 5 minutes after which quick release excess pressure.
4. Remove the chicken and place on your cutting board. When cool enough to handle, shred the chicken with a pair of forks.
5. Add the chicken back into the pot and stir.
6. Press 'Sauté' button and heat thoroughly.

Turkey Quinoa Bowls

Serves: 3

Ingredients:

- ½ pound ground turkey
- ½ teaspoon taco seasoning

- ½ teaspoon salt
- ½ tablespoons oil
- ½ teaspoon dried oregano
- Pepper to taste
- ½ teaspoon salt
- ¾ cup uncooked quinoa
- ¾ cup water
- 2 cloves garlic, grated
- 1 tablespoon soy sauce
- 1 cup frozen green peas
- 1 green onion, finely chopped
- 1 medium onion, chopped
- ½ bell pepper, finely chopped
- 1 tablespoon maple syrup or honey
- 1 cup frozen corn

Directions:

1. Press 'Saute' button. Add oil. When oil is heated, add turkey and cook until it is not pink anymore. Break it simultaneously as it cooks.
2. Add spices, oregano, salt and water and stir. Press 'Cancel' button.
3. Stir in the quinoa. Place bell pepper, onion, garlic, maple syrup and soy sauce on top, without stirring.
4. Close the lid. Select 'Manual' and 'Low Pressure' and timer for 12 minutes.
5. Quick release excess pressure.
6. Stir in corn and peas. Cover and set aside for 10 minutes.
7. Stir in green onions and serve

Turkey Breast with Gravy

Serves: 4

Ingredients:

- 3 ¼ pounds bone-in skin on turkey breast
- 1 cup broth
- 2 cloves garlic, minced
- Salt, pepper and paprika to taste
- 1 teaspoon onion powder
- 1 teaspoon garlic powder
- 1 stick celery, chopped
- 2 tablespoons water
- 1 medium onion, quartered
- 2 teaspoons cornstarch mixed with 2 tablespoons water
- 2 tablespoons thyme, chopped

Directions:

1. Mix together all the spices and salt in a bowl. Sprinkle over turkey. Fill the onions, garlic, thyme, and celery into the turkey breast and place in the instant pot. Add rest of the ingredients.
2. Close the lid. Press 'Poultry' and timer for 30 minutes. Remove the turkey from the pot and place on your cutting board. Slice turkey.
3. Add cornstarch mixture into the pot.
4. Press 'Sauté' button and cook until thick, stirring constantly.
5. Pour gravy over the turkey slices and serve.

Chapter Six: Instant Pot Meat Recipes

Taco Casserole

Serves: 3

Ingredients:

- ¾ pound lean ground beef
- ½ can (from a 10.75 ounces can) condensed cream of onion soup
- ¼ cup water
- 3 corn tortillas (6 inches each), cut into ½ inch strips
- ½ a 14.5 ounces can diced tomatoes with green chilies with liquid
- 0.5 ounce taco seasoning mix
- Salt to taste
- Pepper to taste

To serve:

- 2 green onions, sliced
- ¼ cup sour cream
- ½ cup cheddar cheese, shredded

Directions:

1. Press 'Sauté' button. Add beef and cook until brown. Add rest of the ingredients and stir. Press 'Cancel' button.
2. Close the lid. Select 'Manual' button and timer for 10 minutes. Quick release excess pressure.
3. Sprinkle cheese on top. Cover for 5 minutes. Top with sour cream and green onions and serve.

Hamburger Stew

Serves: 4

Ingredients:

- 2 pounds 90% lean ground beef
- 4 large potatoes, sliced
- 4 medium carrots, sliced
- 4 stalks celery, sliced
- 2 large onions, chopped
- 3 cups frozen peas, thawed
- 2 cans (8 ounces each) tomato sauce
- 2 cans (14.5 ounces each) diced tomatoes with juice
- 4 teaspoons Italian seasoning
- Salt to taste
- Pepper to taste

Directions:

1. Press 'Sauté' button. Add ground beef and cook until brown.
2. Add all the ingredients except peas and stir. Press 'Cancel' button.
3. Select 'Manual' button and timer for 15 minutes. Let the pressure release naturally.
4. Add the peas and stir. Cover and let it sit for a few minutes.
5. Serve warm with toasted bread.

Italian Beef

Serves: 3

Ingredients:

- 1 ¼ pounds beef chuck roast
- 2 tablespoons olive oil
- 1 ½ dry Italian salad dressing mix
- ½ cup water
- 1 tablespoon minced garlic
- 6 ounce jarred pepperoncini peppers
- 4 hamburger buns, split, to serve

Directions:

1. Press 'Sauté' button. Add oil. When the oil is heated, add beef and cook until brown all over.
2. Add rest of the ingredients in a bowl and stir. Pour over the meat.
3. Select 'Manual' button and timer for 15 minutes. Let the pressure release naturally.
4. Shred the beef with a pair of forks and add it back into the pot. Mix well and serve over the bottom halves of the buns. Place toppings of your choice. Cover with top half of the buns and serve.

Apricot Glazed Pork Roast

Serves: 6

Ingredients:

- 9 ounces apricot preserves
- ½ can (from a 10.5 ounces can) condensed chicken broth
- 1 medium onion, chopped
- 2 pounds boneless pork loin
- 1 tablespoon Dijon mustard

Directions:

1. Place roast in the pot.
2. Mix together rest of the ingredients in a bowl and pour over the meat.
3. Close the lid. Select 'Meat /Stew' button.
4. Slice and serve.

Sweet Pulled Pork

Serves: 6

Ingredients:

- 3 pounds pork tenderloin
- 1 ½ cups brown sugar
- 1 ½ cups salsa

Directions:

1. Place pork in the instant pot.
2. Mix together salsa and brown sugar in a bowl and pour over the meat.
3. Close the lid. Select 'Meat /Stew' button.
4. Remove the pork and shred with a pair of forks. Add it back to the pot.
5. Press 'Sauté' button and simmer for a few minutes until slightly thick.
6.

Apple Cider Pork Loin

Serves: 6 – 8

Ingredients:

- 3-3 ½ pounds center cut pork loin
- 2 ½ - 3 cups hard cider
- 3 apples, cored, sliced
- 3 tablespoons olive oil
- 1 large onion, sliced
- 1 ½ tablespoons dry minced onions
- Salt and pepper to taste

Directions:

1. Select 'Sauté' button. Add oil and let it heat.
2. Sprinkle salt, pepper and dry onions over the pork. Place in the instant pot and cook until pork is brown all over. Remove pork and aside on a plate.

3. Add onions to the pot and sauté until translucent. Add rest of the ingredients and pork. Mix well. Press 'Cancel' button.
4. Close the lid. Select 'Meat /Stew' button and timer for 22 minutes. Let the pressure release naturally.
5. Broil for a few minutes for a crispy covering if desired.
6. Slice and serve.

Carnitas Tacos

Serves: 6

Ingredients:

- 1 ½ - 2 pounds pork shoulder butt roast
- ½ can (from a 10 ounces can) diced tomatoes and green chilies, with its liquid
- 1 cup Colby-Monterey Jack cheese, shredded
- 2 teaspoons taco seasoning or to taste
- 6 tortillas, warmed, to serve
- Sour cream to serve

Directions

1. Place pork in the instant pot. Season with taco seasoning. Pour tomatoes over it.
2. Remove the pork with a slotted spoon.
3. Close the lid. Select 'Meat /Stew' button. Let the pressure release naturally.
4. Shred with a pair of forks and add it back to the pot. Heat thoroughly.
5. Place about ½ cup pork on each tortilla. Sprinkle cheese over it. Drizzle some sour cream and serve.

Indian Ground Lamb Curry

Serves: 4 – 5

Ingredients:

- 1 ½ pounds ground lamb
- 3 potatoes, chopped
- 2 onions, chopped
- 4 carrots, chopped
- 1 tablespoon ginger, minced
- 6 cloves garlic, minced
- 1 ½ cup peas
- 2 Serrano peppers, chopped
- 1 ½ teaspoons meat masala
- 2 tablespoons ground coriander
- ½ teaspoon turmeric
- 1 teaspoon chili powder
- 1 ½ cups tomato sauce
- 2 tablespoons ghee
- Salt to taste
- ½ cup water

Directions:

1. Select 'Sauté' button. Add ghee and onions and sauté until golden brown.
2. Add rest of the ingredients and stir. Press 'Cancel' button.
3. Close the lid. Select 'Manual' button and timer for 15 minutes. Let the pressure release naturally.
4. Garnish with cilantro and serve with naan bread or rice.

Chapter Seven: Low Carb Lunch Recipes

Shredded Pork with Beans

Serves: 6

Ingredients:

- 1 ½ pounds pork tenderloins, cut into 3 inch pieces
- ½ jar (from a 24 ounces jar) picante sauce
- 1 ½ cans (15 ounces each) black beans, rinsed, drained

Directions:

1. Add pork and picante sauce into the instant pot and stir.
2. Close the lid. Select 'Manual' button and timer for 20 minutes. Let the pressure release naturally.
3. Add beans and stir. Press 'Sauté' button and simmer for 10 minutes.
4. Serve over rice.

Beef and Mushroom Stew

Serves: 2-3

Ingredients:

- 1 pound beef chuck, chopped into 1 inch cubes
- ½ ounce dry porcini mushrooms
- 12 teaspoons olive oil
- 1 small onion, chopped

- 1 large carrot, sliced into ½ inch rounds
- 1 teaspoon fresh rosemary, minced
- ½ stalk celery, chopped into ½ inch slices
- ½ cup beef stock
- ¼ cup red wine
- Pepper to taste
- Salt to taste
- 1 tablespoon arrowroot
- 1 tablespoon butter

Directions:

1. Press 'Sauté' button. Add oil. When the oil is heated, add beef and sauté until brown. Press 'Cancel' button.
2. Rest of the ingredients except butter, arrowroot and mushrooms and stir. Sprinkle porcini mushrooms on top.
3. Cover and press 'Meat /Stew' button and set timer for 25 minutes. Let the pressure release naturally.
4. Meanwhile, place a small pan over medium heat. Add butter and flour and cook until the flour is slightly off-white in color.
5. Remove from heat. Add a couple of tablespoons of the cooked liquid and whisk well. Transfer into the instant pot and stir constantly.
6. Press 'Sauté' button. Simmer until the stew is thick.
7. Ladle into bowls and serve.

Creamy Cauliflower Soup

Serves: 8

Ingredients:

- 2 onions, chopped
- 8 cups vegetable broth
- Salt to taste
- Pepper to taste

- 2 heads cauliflower, cut into florets
- 1 teaspoon garlic powder

Directions:
1. Add all the ingredients into the instant pot and stir.
2. Select 'Manual' and timer for 15 minutes. Let the pressure release naturally.
3. Blend with an immersion blender until smooth.
4. Ladle into soup bowls and top with low carb toppings if desired and serve.

Poblano Chicken Soup

Serves: 4

Ingredients:
- ¼ cup navy beans, soaked in hot water for an hour
- 2 poblano peppers, chopped
- ½ cup cauliflower florets
- 1 medium onion, diced
- 3 cloves garlic, minced
- ¾ pound chicken breast, chopped into chunks
- ½ teaspoon ground cumin
- ½ teaspoon ground coriander
- 1 teaspoon salt or to taste
- A handful fresh cilantro, chopped
- 1 ½ cups water
- 1 ounce cream cheese, cut into cubes

Directions:
1. Set aside the cream cheese and add rest of the ingredients into the instant pot and stir.
2. Select 'Soup' and timer for 20 minutes. Let the pressure release naturally.
3. Remove chicken with a slotted spoon and place on a plate. Shred with a pair of forks and add it back into the pot.
4. Add cream cheese and stir.

5. Press 'Sauté' button and heat until cream cheese melts and is well blended.

Bacon Cheddar and Broccoli Salad

Serves: 3

Ingredients:
- 1 large head fresh broccoli, chopped into florets
- 1 sweet onion, chopped
- 3 slices bacon, cooked, crumbled
- 2 tablespoons roasted sunflower seeds (optional)
- ¼ cup cheddar cheese, shredded

For the dressing:
- 6 tablespoons mayonnaise
- 1 ½ tablespoons stevia powder
- 1 tablespoon apple cider vinegar

Directions:
1. Add broccoli to the instant pot. Add ½ cup water.
2. Close the lid. Press 'Steam' button and set timer for 3 minutes. Quick release excess pressure.
3. Drain and add to a serving bowl. Add rest of the ingredients for salad and toss well.
4. Whisk together all the ingredients of the dressing in a bowl. Pour over the salad. Toss well and serve.

Egg Salad

Serves: 6

Ingredients:
- 12 eggs
- 2 teaspoons Dijon mustard

- Freshly ground black pepper
- Salt to taste
- 4 tablespoons mayonnaise
- 2 teaspoons lemon juice

<u>To serve:</u>
- Lettuce leaves

Directions:
1. Pour 1 ½ cups water into the instant pot. Place a trivet or steamer basket in it.
2. Place the eggs in the basket.
3. Close the lid. Select 'Manual' button and set timer for 5 minutes.
4. Quick release the excess pressure.
5. Remove eggs and place in a bowl of cold water for a while. Peel and chop the eggs.
6. Add rest of the ingredients and fold gently.
7. Serve over lettuce leaves.

Spinach Frittata

Serves: 6

Ingredients:
- 12 eggs, beaten
- ½ cup diced tomatoes
- 1 small onion, minced
- Pepper to taste
- Salt to taste
- 1 cup chopped spinach
- 1 teaspoon garlic powde

Directions:
1. Grease a heatproof container with some oil.
2. Whisk eggs in a bowl. Add rest of the ingredients and whisk well. Pour into the prepared container. Cover the dish with aluminum foil.

3. Pour 2 cups water into the instant pot. Place a steamer rack in the pot and container on the rack.
4. Close the lid. Press 'Manual' button and timer for 20 minutes.
5. Let the pressure release naturally for 10 minutes after which quick release excess pressure.
6. Let it remain covered for 10 minutes.
7. Run a knife around the edges of the frittata. Invert on to a plate. Broil for a couple of minutes if desired.
8. Slice into wedges and serve.

Chapter Eight: Instant Pot Noodle Recipes

Beef and Spaghetti

Serves: 2 – 3

Ingredients:

- 1 tablespoon olive oil
- 1 clove garlic, mashed
- ½ cup chopped onion
- 1 can (from an 8 ounces can) tomato sauce
- ½ cup water
- ½ pound ground beef
- ½ pound spaghetti
- 1 cup dry red wine
- ½ teaspoon chili powder
- 2 tablespoons shredded parmesan cheese
- Salt to taste

Directions:

1. Select 'Sauté' button. Add oil. When the oil is heated, add beef, onion and garlic and cook until brown.
2. Add rest of the ingredients except cheese and stir. Press 'Cancel' button.
3. Close the lid. Select 'Manual' button and set timer for 6 – 7 minutes depending on how you like it cooked. Quick release the excess pressure.
4. Cover and set Manual option and timer for 7 minutes. Quick release excess pressure. Add cheese and stir.

Mac and Cheese

Serves: 3

Ingredients:

- ½ pound elbow macaroni
- ½ can (from a 12 ounces can) evaporated milk
- 1 ½ cups shredded mild or medium cheddar cheese
- Salt to taste
- 1 ½ tablespoons unsalted butter
- 2 cups water + extra

Directions:

1. Add macaroni, water and about ½ tablespoon salt into an instant pot and stir.
2. Close the lid. Select 'Manual' button and set timer for 4 minutes. Quick release excess pressure.
3. Add evaporated milk, 2 tablespoons water and butter and stir. Stir in the cheddar cheese, a tablespoon at a time. Serve once the cheese melts.

Asian Noodle Bowls

Serves: 2

Ingredients:

- ¼ cup low sodium tamari or soy sauce
- 1 tablespoon almond butter or more to taste
- 1 cup chicken broth
- 1 large carrot, cut into ½ inch thick slices
- 1 tablespoon rice vinegar
- 1 tablespoon erythritol
- ½ pound boneless, skinless chicken breast, cut into bite size pieces
- 4 ounces uncooked brown rice noodles

<u>To serve:</u>

- Green onion slices
- Almonds, slivered

Directions:
1. Add all the ingredients into the instant pot and stir.
2. Close the lid. Select 'Manual' button and set timer for 3 minutes. Quick release excess pressure.
3. Divide into bowls. Top with almonds and green onions and serve.
4.

Spaghetti and Meatballs

Serves: 2 – 3

Ingredients:
- ½ pound cooked, frozen meatballs
- 12 ounces pasta sauce
- ½ tablespoon olive oil
- 4 ounces uncooked spaghetti, break into 2 halves
- 1 ½ cups water

For garnishing:
- Parmesan cheese
- Fresh basil

Directions:
1. Place meatballs in the instant pot, in a single layer. Scatter spaghetti over the meatballs.
2. Pour oil all over the spaghetti. Mix together water and sauce into a bowl and pour over the spaghetti.
3. Close the lid. Select 'Manual' button and set timer for 4 minutes. Quick release excess pressure.
4. Add basil and cheese and mix well.

Chicken Alfredo

Serves: 2

Ingredients:

- ½ pound chicken thighs, skinless, boneless, cubed
- ½ jar (from a 16 ounces jar) Alfredo sauce
- Salt to taste
- Pepper to taste
- ½ teaspoon minced garlic
- 1 cup water
- 4 ounces dry fettuccini or whole wheat linguine, broken
- ½ tablespoon olive oil
- Grated parmesan cheese to serve

Directions:

1. Season the chicken with salt and pepper.
2. Press 'Sauté' button. Add oil. When the oil is heated, garlic and chicken and cook until light brown all over.
3. Spread the pasta over the chicken. Pour Alfredo sauce over it. Close the lid without stirring the contents.
5. Close the lid. Select 'Manual' button and set timer for 9 minutes. Quick release excess pressure.
4. Stir now. Garnish with Parmesan cheese and serve with a side dish of your choice.

Enchilada Pasta

Serves: 2

Ingredients:

- 4 ounces penne pasta
- ¾ cup broth
- 6 ounces enchilada sauce

- 1 pound ground beef or turkey
- 1 cup shredded cheese
- 1 tablespoon taco seasoning
- ¼ cup sour cream
- ½ can black olives, pitted
- Fresh cilantro to garnish

Directions:
1. Select 'Sauté' button. Add meat and taco seasoning and cook until brown. Press 'Cancel' button.
2. Add broth, pasta and sauce and stir.
3. Close the lid. Select 'Manual' button and set timer for 4 minutes. Quick release excess pressure. Add sour cream and stir.
4. Sprinkle cheese and olives on top and serve.

Chicken Sausage Pasta

Serves: 3

Ingredients:
- 3 teaspoons olive oil
- 1 small onion, chopped
- ½ can (from a 28 ounces can) crushed tomatoes in puree
- ½ pound lean ground chicken sausage
- 8 ounces bow tie pasta
- Red pepper flakes to taste
- 1 ¾ cups water
- 1 clove garlic, crushed
- ½ teaspoon dried basil
- ½ teaspoon salt
- ½ teaspoon pepper

Directions:

1. Press 'Saute' button. Add oil. When the oil is heated, add sausage, garlic and onion and cook until onion turns translucent.
2. Stir in the remaining ingredients.
3. Close the lid. Select 'Manual' button and set timer for 5 minutes. Quick release excess pressure.

Broccoli & Cheddar Pasta

Serves: 2 – 4

Ingredients:

- ½ pound pasta
- 8 ounces cheddar cheese, shredded
- ½ cup milk or half and half
- 2 cups water
- 8 ounces frozen broccoli
- 1 ½ pounds grilled chicken, shredded (optional)
- Salt and pepper, as per taste

Directions:

1. Add water, pasta and broccoli into the instant pot.
2. Close the lid. Select 'Manual' button and timer for 4 minutes. Quick release excess pressure.
3. Press 'Sauté' button. Add milk, cheese, seasoning and chicken. Stir and simmer until thoroughly heated.

Chapter Nine: Instant Pot Vegetarian Recipes

Creamed Corn

Serves: 4

Ingredients:

- 2 cans (15 ounces each) corn kernels
- 1 ½ tablespoons butter, diced
- Salt to taste
- Freshly cracked pepper to taste
- 4 ounces cream cheese, diced
- ½ tablespoon honey or sugar (optional)
- 3 tablespoons milk

Directions:

1. Add all the ingredients into the instant pot and stir.
2. Close the lid. Select 'Manual' button and timer for 6 minutes. Quick release excess pressure.

Enchilada Quinoa

Serves: 2

Ingredients:

- ½ can (from a 15 ounces can) black beans, drained, rinsed
- 1 can (15 ounces) mild or medium red enchilada sauce, divided

- ½ can (from a 15 ounces can) yellow corn, drained, rinsed
- ½ can (from a 15 ounces) can diced fire roasted tomatoes with green chilies
- ½ cup quinoa, uncooked
- 2 ounces cream cheese
- ¼ cup water
- ½ cup shredded Mexican cheese
- 2 tablespoons chopped fresh cilantro
- 2 tablespoons sour cream
- 2 tomatoes, chopped

Directions:
1. Add all the ingredients except cheese into the instant pot and stir.
2. Sprinkle cheese on top.
3. Press 'Rice' button. When done, fluff with a fork. Serve with toppings of your choice.

Instant Pot Rice and Beans

Serves: 3

Ingredients:
- 1 cup dry brown rice
- 1 cup dry red kidney beans
- ½ cup salsa
- 1 ½ cups vegetable broth
- A handful fresh cilantro, chopped + extra to garnish
- 1 ½ cups water

Directions:
1. Add beans, rice, water and broth into the instant pot and stir.
2. Pour salsa on top. Sprinkle cilantro. Do not stir.
3. Close the lid. Select 'Manual' button and timer for 25 minutes. Let the pressure release naturally for 10 minutes after which quick release excess pressure.

4. Stir now. Garnish with some cilantro and serve.

Peas Risotto

Serves: 2

Ingredients:

- 1 cup Arborio rice
- 1 medium onion, chopped
- ¾ cup frozen peas
- 3 cups chicken or vegetable broth
- 3 tablespoons parmesan cheese
- 3 tablespoons butter
- 2 cloves garlic, minced
- Salt to taste
- Pepper to taste

Directions:

1. Select 'Sauté' button. Add butter to instant pot. When butter melts, add onions and garlic and sauté until onion turns pink.
2. Add rice and sauté for 2 minutes. Add ¾ cup broth and mix well. Cook until dry. Press 'Cancel' button.
3. Add remaining broth and stir.
4. Close the lid. Select 'Manual' button and timer for 5 minutes. Add, salt, pepper, peas and cheese. Mix well. Close the lid and let it rest for 10 minutes.
5. Stir and serve.

Vegetarian Chili

Serves: 8

Ingredients:

- 2 cans (15 ounces each) stewed tomatoes
- 2 cans (6 ounces each) tomato paste
- 2 teaspoons ground cumin
- Salt to taste
- Pepper to taste
- 2 cans (15 ounces each) unsalted pinto beans, with its liquid
- 1 tablespoon chili powder or to taste

Directions:

1. Add all the ingredients into the instant pot and stir.
2. Close the lid. Select 'Manual' button and timer for 8 minutes. Quick release excess pressure. Serve with toppings of your choice.

Chipotle-Orange Broccoli & Tofu

Serves: 8

Ingredients:

- 2 packages (14 ounces each) extra-firm water packed tofu, pat dried, cut into cubes
- 6 tablespoons canola oil, divided
- 2 tablespoons minced chipotle is adobo sauce
- Salt to taste
- 12 cups broccoli florets
- 1 cup chopped cilantro
- 2 cups orange juice

Directions:

1. Press 'Sauté' button. Add 4 tablespoons oil. When the oil is heated, add tofu and sprinkle some salt. Cook until brown all over. Remove with a slotted spoon and set aside on a plate.
2. Add 2 tablespoons oil. Stir broccoli for a minute. Press 'Cancel' button.
3. Add orange juice, salt and chipotle and stir.

4. Close the lid. Press 'Steam' button and set timer for 3 minutes. Quick release excess pressure.
5. Add tofu and cilantro. Stir and serve.

Coconut Curry

Serves: 6 – 8

Ingredients:
- 2 cans coconut milk
- 1 large head broccoli, cut into florets
- 4 – 5 cups cubed vegetables of your choice
- 2 cans (15 ounces each) chickpeas, rinsed, drained
- 1 onion, chopped
- 4 tablespoons red curry paste
- 1 tablespoon cornstarch mixed with 4 tablespoons water
- Salt to taste

Directions:
1. Press 'Sauté' button. Add oil. When the oil is heated, add onions and sauté until translucent. Press 'Cancel' button.
2. Add rest of the ingredients except cornstarch mixture and stir.
3. Close the lid. Select 'Manual' button and timer for 8 minutes. Quick release excess pressure.
4. Press 'Sauté' button. Add cornstarch mixture and stir constantly until thick.
5. Serve over rice.

Chapter Ten: Instant Pot Seafood Recipes

Beer Potato Fish

Serves: 2

Ingredients:

- ½ pound fish fillets
- ½ cup beer
- ½ tablespoons oil
- 2 medium potatoes, cubed
- ½ red pepper, sliced
- ½ tablespoon oyster sauce
- Salt to taste
- ½ tablespoon rock candy

Directions:
1. Add all the ingredients into the instant pot.
2. Close the lid. Press 'Manual' button and timer for 10 minutes. Let the pressure release naturally. Stir and serve.

Fish with Orange and Ginger Sauce

Serves: 2

Ingredients:

- 2 fish fillets, pat dried
- 2 spring onions, sliced
- Juice of ½ orange
- Zest of ½ orange, grated
- 1 inch fresh ginger, peeled, minced
- 1 tablespoon olive oil
- ½ cup fish stock or white wine
- Salt to taste
- Pepper to taste

To serve:
- Salad greens

Directions:
1. Rub fillets with olive oil. Sprinkle salt and pepper.
2. Add rest of the ingredients into the instant pot and stir.
3. Place a steamer basket in the pot. Place fish in the basket.
4. Close the lid. Select 'Manual' button and timer for 7 minutes. Quick release excess pressure.
5. Place fish over a bed of salad greens. Pour sauce over it and serve.

Garlic Butter Tilapia

Serves: 2

Ingredients:
- 2 tilapia fillets
- Salt to taste
- Pepper to taste
- 1 tablespoon garlic compound butter, chopped into small cubes

Directions:

1. Place a large sheet of foil on your countertop. Lay the fillets in the middle of the foil. Sprinkle salt and pepper over it. Place butter cubes on the fillets.
2. Wrap foil all around the fish. Seal it well. Place in the instant pot.
3. Close lid. Select 'Slow cook' button and timer for 2 hours.

Peas with Cod

Serves: 2

Ingredients:

- ½ pound cod fillets, cut into 2 parts
- ½ cup wine
- ¼ pound peas
- 2 cloves garlic, halved
- 2 tablespoons chopped fresh parsley
- ¼ teaspoon dried oregano
- 2 tablespoons chopped almonds
- Salt to taste
- Pepper to taste

Directions:

1. Add almonds, paprika, salt, garlic and oregano to the small blender jar and pulse until finely chopped. Transfer into a bowl. Add wine and stir. Set aside.
2. Pour 1 ½ cups water into the instant pot. Place a steamer rack in it. Place fillets on the steamer rack.
3. Close lid. Select 'Manual' button and timer for 2 minutes.
4. Quick release excess pressure. Remove cod and set aside.
5. Add peas into the pot.
6. Close lid. Select 'Manual' button and timing for 2 Steam option and timer for 5 minutes.
7. Place peas over cod. Pour almond mixture over it and serve.

Sweet and Sour Shrimp

Serves: 2

Ingredients:

- 1 tablespoon olive oil
- 1 cup chopped bell pepper
- 1 tablespoon soy sauce
- 1 tablespoon honey
- 1 small onion, chopped
- 8 ounces frozen shrimp
- 1 tablespoon ketchup

Directions:

1. Press 'Saute' button. Add oil. When the oil is heated, add onions and cook for a couple of minutes.
2. Stir in the bell peppers and cook until onions turn translucent.
3. Add rest of the ingredients and mix well. Press 'Cancel' button.
4. Close lid. Select 'Manual' button and timer for 2 minutes.
5. Quick release excess pressure. Stir and serve.

Spicy Mussels in Tomato Gravy

Serves: 4 – 6

Ingredients:

- 4 pounds mussels, scrubbed, debearded
- 4 tablespoons olive oil
- 4 minced teaspoons garlic
- 2 onions, chopped
- 1 teaspoon red pepper flakes
- 1 cup chicken broth
- 2 cans (14 ounces each) diced tomatoes

- 4 teaspoons dried oregano
- Salt to taste

Directions:

1. Select 'Sauté' button. Add oil. When the oil is heated, add onions and sauté until translucent. Add garlic and sauté until fragrant.
2. Add rest of the ingredients and stir well. Press 'Cancel' button.
3. Close lid. Select 'Manual' button and timer for 1 minute.
4. Quick release excess pressure. Stir and discard any mussels that do not open. Serve hot.

Chapter Eleven: Instant Snacks Recipes

BBQ Chicken Drummies

Serves: 6

Ingredients:

- 1 ½ pounds chicken drummies, thawed, pat dried
- 2 tablespoons honey
- 1 tablespoon chili sauce
- ¾ cup barbecue sauce
- 2 cloves garlic, minced
- Pepper to taste

Directions:

1. Add all the ingredients into the instant pot and stir.
2. Close the lid. Select 'Poultry' button. Let the pressure release naturally for 10 minutes after which quick release excess pressure. Stir and serve.

Asian Chinese Boiled Peanuts

Serves:

Ingredients:

- 2 pounds large raw peanuts, with shells

- 2 chunks rock sugar
- 4 star anise
- 6 cloves garlic
- 4 sticks cinnamon
- 8 dried red chili peppers (optional)

Directions:
1. Add all the ingredients to instant pot. Cover with water. Place a heavy plate or a trivet over the peanuts, as they tend to float.
2. Close lid. Select 'Manual' button and timer for 80 minutes. Let the pressure release naturally.
3. Cool, shell peanuts and serve.

Five Spice Chicken Wings

Serves: 8

Ingredients:
- 8 chicken wings, chop the wing tips, chop each wing into 2 pieces
- 2 teaspoons butter, melted
- 6 tablespoons sugar free plum sauce
- 1 teaspoon five spice powder or to taste
- Salt to taste
- Sliced green onions to serve

Directions:
1. Press 'Sauté' button and spray some cooking spray. Add chicken and cook until brown.
2. Add rest of the ingredients and mix well. Press 'Cancel' button.
3. Close the lid. Select 'Slow cook' button and set timer for 1 ½ - 2 hours.
4. Stir well. Garnish with green onions and serve.
5.

Lettuce Wraps

Serves: 4

Ingredients:

- 1 tablespoon olive oil
- 1 carrot, chopped
- 4 – 5 tablespoons water
- ½ cup soy sauce
- ¼ teaspoon red chili flakes
- 1 teaspoon minced ginger
- ½ pound ground pork
- ½ bunch green onions, sliced
- ½ cup hoisin sauce
- 4 ounces canned water chestnuts, drained
- 8 Bibb lettuce leaves, to serve

Directions:

1. Select 'Sauté' button. Add oil. When the oil is heated, add pork, green onions and carrot and sauté for 5 minutes. Press 'Cancel' button.
2. Add water and stir the bottom of the pot to remove any browned bits that may be stuck.
3. Place water chestnuts over the pork.
4. Add rest of the ingredients into a bowl and stir. Pour over the water chestnut layer, without stirring.
5. Close the lid. Select 'Manual' button and timer for 2 minutes. Let the pressure release naturally.
6. Place lettuce leaves on a serving platter. Divide the mixture among the lettuce leaves. Wrap and serve.

Corn on the Cob

Serves: 2

Ingredients:

- 2 ears corn, remove the husk

To serve: Optional

- Melted butter
- Lemon juice
- Salt and pepper
- Sauce of your choice etc.

Directions:

1. Pour 1 ½ cups water into the instant pot. Place a steamer basket or rack in it.
2. Place corn cob on the steamer rack.
3. Close the lid. Select 'Manual' button and timer for 15 minutes.
4. Serve with suggested serving options.

BBQ Smoked Sausage

Serves: 10

Ingredients:

- 1 pound smoked breakfast sausages, cut into 1 inch pieces
- ¼ tablespoon brown sugar
- Sweet BBQ sauce as required
- 1 teaspoon lemon juice

Directions:

1. Place sausages in the instant pot. Cover with water.
2. Close the lid. Select 'Manual' button and timer for 10 minutes. Quick release excess pressure. Drain and transfer into bowl.
3. Mix together rest of the ingredients in a bowl and pour over sausages. Mix well. Insert toothpicks in each piece and serve.

Cocktail Meatballs

Serves: 10

Ingredients:

- 1 pound appetizer size, cooked, frozen meatballs, thawed
- 1 cup chili sauce or cocktail sauce
- 8 – 9 ounces grape jelly
- ¼ cup water

Directions:

1. Mix together water, jelly and chili sauce in a bowl.
2. Place the meatballs in the instant pot. Pour the mixture over it.
3. Close the lid. Select 'Manual' button and timer for 7 minutes. Quick release excess pressure. If there is too much liquid in the pot, press 'Sauté' button and simmer until thick.
4. Transfer into bowl. Mix until well coated.
5. Insert toothpicks and serve.

Chicken Nachos

Serves: 4

Ingredients:

- ¾ pound, boneless, skinless, medium chicken breasts
- 1 cup salsa
- ½ tablespoon taco seasoning or to taste
- A handful fresh cilantro
- Juice of a lime

To serve:

- Tortilla chips, as required
- 1 cup shredded cheddar cheese
- Chopped avocado
- Sour cream etc.

Directions:

1. Sprinkle taco seasoning over the chicken and place in the instant pot. Add salsa, lime juice and cilantro and mix well.
2. Close the lid. Select 'Manual' button and timer for 8 minutes. Quick release excess pressure. Shred the chicken with a pair of forks. Add chicken back into the pot and stir. If there is too much liquid in the pot, press 'Sauté' button and simmer until thick.
3. Set an oven to broiler mode. Place a sheet of parchment paper on a baking sheet. Place the tortilla chips over it, in a single layer. Place chicken over the chips. Sprinkle cheese on top. Broil for a few minutes until cheese melts.
4. Drizzle sour cream on top. Garnish with avocado and any other toppings of your choice and serve.

Little Smokies

Serves: 8

Ingredients:

- 2 packages (14 ounces each) little smokies
- ½ cup pineapple juice
- 1 cup chili sauce or to taste
- ¼ cup brown sugar

Directions:

1. Add all the ingredients except smokies into the instant pot and stir well.
2. Add little smokies and mix well.

3. Close the lid. Select 'Manual' button and timer for 20 minutes. Quick release excess pressure. Transfer into a bowl and cool for a while. Insert toothpicks and serve.

Garlic and Butter Mushrooms

Serves: 6 – 8

Ingredients:

- 4 tablespoons olive oil
- 4 – 6 tablespoons butter
- 1 teaspoon minced thyme
- Salt to taste
- 2 pounds button mushrooms
- 4 – 5 teaspoons minced garlic
- A handful fresh parsley, chopped, to garnish

Directions:

1. Press 'Sauté' button. Add oil. When the oil is heated, place the mushrooms in the pot, with the stem side up. Do not stir and cook until brown. Cook the mushrooms in batches if required.
2. Add rest of the ingredients and stir. Press 'Cancel' button.
3. Close the lid. Select 'Manual' button and timer for 12 minutes. Quick release excess pressure.
4. If there is more liquid in the pot, press 'Sauté' button and simmer until nearly dry. Transfer into a bowl and cool for a while. Garnish with parsley.
5. Insert toothpicks and serve.

Instant Pot Popcorns

Serves: 2 – 3

Ingredients:

- 1 tablespoon ghee or unrefined coconut oil
- ¼ cup popcorn kernels
- ½ teaspoon salt
- 1 tablespoon chocolate or vanilla protein powder (optional)

Directions:

1. Press 'Sauté' button. Add ghee and let the pot heat. Add salt and stir the oil.
2. Drop 2 -3 corn kernels in the pot. When they pop, add rest of the popcorn kernels and stir. Cover with a see-through lid. Leave a small gap between the lid and the pot.
3. The corn will begin to pop. When the popping reduces, switch off the pot and let it cool for a couple of minutes.
4. Toss well and serve.
5. If you want flavored popcorn, add chocolate or vanilla protein powder or any other flavor of your choice like Parmesan cheese, Cajun seasoning etc. and toss well.

Queso Dip

Serves: 8 – 10

Ingredients:

- 3 ½ cups cooked ground Italian sausages
- 8 cups chunk pasteurized processed Queso Blanco cheese
- 2 cans (10 ounces each) chopped tomatoes with green chilies
- ½ cup wate

Directions:

1. Add all ingredients into the instant pot and stir.
2. Select 'Manual' button and timer for 5 minutes. Let the pressure release naturally for 10 minutes after which quick release excess pressure.
3. Stir well.

4. Serve with tortilla chips, pita wedges, crackers, vegetable sticks etc.
5.

Spinach and Artichoke Dip

Serves: 4

Ingredients:

- 2 cans (14 ounces each) artichoke hearts, drained, coarsely chopped
- 2 packages (10 ounces each) frozen chopped spinach, thawed, drained
- 2 cups light mayonnaise
- 2 cups grated mozzarella cheese
- 2 cups grated parmesan
- 1 cup sour cream
- ¼ teaspoon cayenne pepper
- ½ teaspoon garlic salt
- Pepper to taste

Directions:

1. Add all ingredients to the instant pot and stir.
2. Select 'Manual' button and timer for 10 minutes. Quick release excess pressure.
3. Stir and cool. Serve with pita wedges, tortilla chips, crackers, vegetable sticks etc.

Buffalo Chicken Dip

Serves: 10 - 15

Ingredients:

- ½ package (from an 8 ounce package) cream cheese, softened
- 2 chicken breasts, skinless, boneless
- 1 ½ tablespoons butter

- 1 tablespoon water
- ½ cup shredded mozzarella cheese
- ½ cup cheddar
- 2 tablespoons ranch dressing
- 6 cups hot sauce

Directions:

1. Add all the ingredients into the instant pot and stir.
2. Select 'Manual' button and timer for 10 minutes. Quick release excess pressure.
3. Shred the chicken with a pair of forks and add it back into the pot. Mix well.
4. Serve warm with toasted bread sticks or celery sticks or crackers.

Sausage Dip

Serves: 10

Ingredients:

- ½ pound ground turkey or pork sausage, crumbled
- ½ can (from a 14 ounces can) crushed tomatoes with its liquid
- 1 block (8 ounces) cream cheese or Neufchatel cheese

Directions:

1. Add water and turkey into the instant pot and stir.
2. Select 'Manual' button and timer for 4 minutes. Quick release excess pressure. Discard fat.
3. Press 'Sauté' button. Add cream cheese, tomatoes, salt and pepper and mix well.

Chapter Twelve: Instant Pot Dessert Recipes

Blueberry Pudding

Serves: 12 – 15

Ingredients:

- 2 cups plain flour
- 1 teaspoon salt
- 5 tablespoons dried breadcrumbs
- 2 eggs, beaten
- 3 teaspoons baking powder
- 1 pound blueberries
- 1 cup chopped butter
- 1 cup granulated sugar
- 10 ounces milk
- Whipped cream to serve

Directions:

1. Add all the dry ingredients into a bowl. Add butter and mix. Add milk and eggs and beat well. Add blueberries and stir. Transfer into a baking dish greased with some butter.
2. Place a trivet inside the instant pot. Pour 2 cups of water. Place dish over the trivet.
3. Cover the pot with a transparent lid. Select 'Steam' and timer for 15 minutes.

4. Close the lid. Select 'Manual' button and timer for 35 minutes. Quick release excess pressure. Loosen the pudding by passing a knife around the edges and invert onto a plate. Cut into wedges.
5. Serve topped with cream.

Chai Spiced Pears

Serves: 4

Ingredients:

- 4 ripe, medium sized pears, peeled, cored
- 2 sticks cinnamon
- 1 ½ cups fresh orange juice
- ½ inch piece fresh ginger, peeled, sliced
- 3 tablespoons maple syrup
- 4 pods cardamom
- 1 teaspoon ground cinnamon, to garnish
- ¼ cup walnuts, roughly chopped, to garnish

Directions:

1. Add all the ingredients except walnuts and ground cinnamon to the instant pot.
2. Close the lid. Select 'Manual' button and timer for 8 minutes. Quick release excess pressure.
3. Sprinkle cinnamon and walnuts and serve warm.

Chocolate Fudge

Serves: 25 - 30

Ingredients:

- 4 cups semi-select chocolate chips
- 2 cans (14 ounces) condensed milk
- 2 cups milk chocolate chips
- 4 tablespoons butter
- A pinch of sea salt
- ½ teaspoon vanilla extract

Directions:

1. Add all the ingredients to the instant pot. Mix well.
2. Press 'Saute' button. Whisk constantly until well incorporated. Press 'Keep Warm' button. Let it remain in this mode until melted completely. Whisk well.
3. Transfer the mixture into a greased tin. Cover and refrigerate until the fudge is set.

Pineapple Cake

Serves: 8

Ingredients:

- ½ box (from a 14 ounces box) yellow cake mix
- ½ can (from a 14 ounces can) pineapple pieces, drained
- 2 ounces unsalted butter + extra to grease

Directions:

1. Make batter of the cake according to the instructions given on the package.
2. Grease a cake pan with a little butter.
3. Place a layer of pineapple slices in the pan. Pour batter in the dish.
4. Cover the dish with foil.
5. Place a trivet inside the instant pot. Pour 2 cups of water into the pot. Place the dish on the trivet.
6. Close the lid. Select 'Manual' button and timer for 17-20 minutes.
7. Uncover and cool. Invert on to a plate. Slice and serve.

Raspberry Curd

Serves: 3 – 4

Ingredients:

- 1 egg yolk
- 6 ounces raspberries
- 1 tablespoon lemon juice
- 1 tablespoon butter
- ½ cup sugar

Directions:

1. Stir together raspberries, sugar and lemon juice in the instant pot.
2. Close the lid. Select 'Manual' button and timer for 1 minute. Let the pressure release naturally for 5 minutes after which quick release excess pressure.
3. Strain the raspberries through a fine wire mesh strainer. Discard the seeds.
4. Whisk the yolk. Add the strained raspberry pulp into the bowl of yolk a little at a timer and whisk well each time. Pour into the instant pot.
5. Select 'Sauté' button. Stir constantly for a few minutes. Switch off the pot. Whisk in the butter. Stir and pour into a serving bowl. Chill and serve.

Chocolate Fondue

Serves: 6

Ingredients:

- 12 ounces chocolate, chopped into chunks
- ½ teaspoon vanilla extract
- 7 ounces fresh cream

Directions:

1. Pour 2 cups of water to the instant pot. Place the steamer rack inside the pot.
2. Add chocolate and cream into a heatproof bowl. Place the bowl on the rack.
3. Close the lid. Select 'Manual' button and timer for 2 minutes. Let the pressure release naturally.
4. Add vanilla and whisk vigorously until smooth. Serve with fruits or cookies or pretzels.

Quick Custard

Serves: 8

Ingredients:

- 8 eggs, beaten

- 4 cups milk, warm
- ½ teaspoon ground nutmeg
- 2/3 cup sugar

Directions:

1. Add all the ingredients into a bowl and whisk until sugar dissolves.
2. Pour into ramekins. Cover ramekins with foil.
3. Pour 2 cups water in the instant pot and place a steamer rack over it. Place the cups on the rack. You can stack them.
4. Close the lid. Select 'Manual' button and timer for 7 minutes. Quick release the excess pressure. Chill and serve.
5.

Crème Brulee

Serves: 8

Ingredients:

- 8 large egg yolks
- 2/3 cup granulated sugar
- 2 teaspoons vanilla extract
- 4 tablespoons very fine sugar, to top
- A pinch of fine salt
- 3 cups heavy cream

Directions:

1. Whisk together in a bowl, yolks, sugar and salt. Add cream and vanilla and whisk until well blended.
2. Strain the entire mixture into a large measuring cup with a pout. Pour this mixture into custard cups or ramekins. Cover the cups with aluminum foil.
3. Place a trivet in the instant pot. Pour about 1-½ cups of water into the pot.
4. Place the cups on the trivet.
5. Close the lid. Select 'Manual' button and timer for 7 minutes. Let the pressure release naturally.
6. Remove the cups after a while. Uncover and cool.

7. Serve warm or chilled. Sprinkle with fine sugar on top. Caramelize with a culinary torch until golden brown on top.

Fruit Cake

Serves: 20

Ingredients:
- 3 cups gluten-free flour
- 3 cups orange juice
- 6 teaspoons baking powder
- ¾ cup candied fruit mix
- ¾ cup unsalted mixed nuts
- ½ teaspoon grated orange zest

Directions:
1. Grease the instant pot with oil.
2. Add all the ingredients into a bowl and whisk well.
3. Pour into the instant pot.
4. Close the lid. Press 'Rice' button. Cool completely. Slice and serve.

Winter Fruit Compote

Serves: about 20

Ingredients:
- 6 cups frozen cranberries
- ½ cup thawed orange juice concentrate
- 1 cup chopped dried apricots
- 1 cup chopped, toasted walnuts
- 1 1/3 cups packed brown sugar

- 4 tablespoons raspberry vinegar
- 1 cup golden raisins

Directions:

1. Add cranberries, orange juice, brown sugar and vinegar into the instant pot and stir.
2. Close the lid. Select 'Manual' button and timer for 3 minutes. Let the pressure release naturally for 5 minutes after which quick release excess pressure.
3. Add raisins, apricots and walnuts and stir.

Chapter Thirteen: Instant pot Low Carb Desserts

Thai Coconut Pandan Custard

Serves: 8

Ingredients:
- 2 cups coconut milk, unsweetened
- 6-8 drops pandan extract
- 6 eggs
- 2/3 cup truvia baking blend or swerve

Directions:
1. Add all the ingredients into a heatproof container and whisk well. Cover the dish with aluminum foil.
2. Pour 2 cups water into the instant pot. Place a trivet in it. Place the bowl on the trivet.
3. Close the lid. Press 'Manual' button and timer for 30 minutes. Let the pressure release naturally.
4. Chill and serve.
5.

Coffee Roll Egg Custard

Serves: 8

Ingredients:
- 6 eggs
- ¼ teaspoon salt
- 1 teaspoon ground cinnamon

- 1 cup almond milk, unsweetened
- 2 cups strong brewed coffee
- 4 tablespoons vanilla whey protein powder
- 1 teaspoon instant espresso
- 1 teaspoon cinnamon liquid stevia or vanilla
- 1 cup heavy cream

Directions:
1. Add almond milk, brewed coffee and cream into a saucepan. Place the saucepan over low heat. Turn off the heat when it begins to steam.
2. Add rest of the ingredients into a mixing bowl and whisk well.
3. Add a little of the almond milk mixture into the mixing bowl and beat well.
4. Add the remaining almond mixture in a thin stream beating constantly, until well combined.
5. Divide and pour the mixture into 8 ramekins. Cover with foil.
6. Pour 2 cups water into the instant pot. Place the ramekins in it.
7. Close the lid. Press 'Manual' button and timer for 60-90 minutes or until set.
8. Chill and serve.

Peanut Butter Chocolate Cheesecake

Serves: 8

Ingredients:
- 6 eggs
- 32 ounces cream cheese
- 2 tablespoons cocoa
- 4 tablespoons powdered peanut butter
- 1 cup swerve sugar substitute
- 2 teaspoons vanilla extract
- Whipped cream and peanut butter to top

Directions:

1. Add all the ingredients into the blender and blend until smooth. Pour into 8 ramekins. Cover with foil.
2. Pour 2 cups of water into the pot. Place a steamer rack in in and the ramekins over it.
3. Close the lid. Press 'Manual' button and timer for 15 minutes. Let the pressure release naturally.
4. Chill and serve.

Vanilla Bean Cheesecake

Serves: 4

Ingredients:

- 8 ounces cultured cream cheese
- 1 small vanilla bean, scraped
- 1 large egg
- ¼ cup swerve sweetener
- ½ teaspoon vanilla extract
- Sugar free red raspberry chia jam to top (optional)

Directions:

1. Add all the ingredients into a blender and blend until smooth. Pour into a small spring form pan.
2. Pour 2 cups water in the instant pot. Place a steamer rack in it. Place the pan over the rack.
3. Close the lid. Select 'Manual' button and set timer for 20 minutes. Let the pressure release naturally.
4. Chill and serv

Conclusion

On that note, we have come to the end of this book. I thank you once again for choosing this book and I sincerely hope you found the book informative.

The instant pot can be easily called as a modern day kitchen wonder, which makes cooking extremely easy. The best part about the instant pot is you don't have to stand by a hot stove for hours in the kitchen to make a healthy home cooked meal. All you need to do is prep your ingredients and toss them in the instant pot and wait and watch it perform its magic.

Food cooked in an instant pot is cooked under pressure and hence doesn't lose its essential nutrition and all the flavours are locked too. The recipes mentioned in this book are all extremely easy to prepare and the ingredients used are also locally available in any farmers market. For best result, try to use as much as fresh and organic produce. Also, eat fresh and store your food properly for further use if you are into meal prepping.

If you follow the recipes as per directions, you can be rest assured that you will be a master chef and can prepare delicious healthy meals at home. So without any further ado, let's get started.

www.ingramcontent.com/pod-product-compliance
Lightning Source LLC
Chambersburg PA
CBHW071745080526
44588CB00013B/2161